The voice of mental health

The**inspirational**series™
Overcoming adversity and thriving

Burlesque Or Bust
Bringing My Mental Health to Heel
BY SAPPHIRA

We are proud to introduce The**inspirational**series™. Part of the Trigger family of innovative mental health books, The**inspirational**series™ tells the stories of the people who have battled and beaten mental health issues. For more information visit: www.triggerpublishing.com

THE AUTHOR

Sapphira (real name Priscilla Silcock née Tonkin) is an Australian burlesque entrepreneur, singer/songwriter and teacher who believes in positivity. Following her recovery from a severe mental illness 20 years ago, she founded Sapphira's Showgirls, an academy that empowers women through self-expression. Sapphira supports several charities with her fundraiser, #BurlesqueAPeel. She is the founder of the Ibiza Burlesque Festival and offers sound healing sessions as a certified Soul Voice® Practitioner.

Sapphira began writing under her original name in Melbourne in 1998, and went on to broaden her career in print as a music journalist. Now, Sapphira is preparing to release her first album, *Mistress*, produced by her husband Tonestepa, and is writing her first poetry book, *Soliloquy*, illustrated by Sir Charles Billich.

First published in Great Britain 2018 by Trigger

Trigger is a trading style of Shaw Callaghan Ltd & Shaw Callaghan 23 USA, INC.

The Foundation Centre

Navigation House, 48 Millgate, Newark

Nottinghamshire NG24 4TS UK

www.triggerpublishing.com

British Library Cataloguing in Publication Data

A CIP catalogue record for this book is available upon request from the British Library

ISBN: 978-1-912478-42-2

This book is also available in the following formats:

MOBI: 978-1-912478-45-3
EPUB: 978-1-912478-43-9
PDF: 978-1-912478-44-6
AUDIO: 978-1-912478-86-6

Cover design and typeset by Fusion Graphic Design Ltd

Printed and bound in Great Britain by Clays Ltd, Elcograf S.p.A.

Paper from responsible sources

www.triggerpublishing.com

Thank you for purchasing this book.
You are making an incredible difference.

Proceeds from all Trigger books go directly to
The Shaw Mind Foundation, a global charity that focuses
entirely on mental health. To find out more about
The Shaw Mind Foundation visit,
www.shawmindfoundation.org

MISSION STATEMENT

Our goal is to make help and support available for every
single person in society, from all walks of life.
We will never stop offering hope. These are our promises.

Trigger and The Shaw Mind Foundation

A NOTE FROM THE SERIES EDITOR

The Inspirational range from Trigger brings you genuine stories about our authors' experiences with mental health problems.

Some of the stories in our Inspirational range will move you to tears. Some will make you laugh. Some will make you feel angry, or surprised, or uplifted. Hopefully they will all change the way you see mental health problems.

These are stories we can all relate to and engage with. Stories of people experiencing mental health difficulties and finding their own ways to overcome them with dignity, humour, perseverance and spirit.

Sapphira's story is an intriguing journey from a strict religious upbringing, navigating a drug induced psychotic episode, to discover her own identity. *Burlesque or Bust* is an inspiring tale which shows readers that is possible to come back from an episode of severe mental illness –including a stay in a psychiatric hospital - and go on to follow your dreams.

This is our Inspirational range. These are our stories. We hope you enjoy them. And most of all, we hope that they will educate and inspire you. That's what this range is all about.

Lauren Callaghan

*This book is dedicated to my husband
and our friend Marc Durif,
My sister, who is my guiding star,
Jack the Bear, who is my guardian angel.*

Disclaimer: Some names and identifying details have been changed to protect the privacy of individuals.

When I dance you see yourself
I am your mirror
When I sing you hear your song
I echo your love
When I write you read your truth,
I channel your story
I am you
You are me
We are one

Mirror Image,
Sapphira

CHAPTER 1

BREATHE

Is it nature or nurture? I pondered silently, holding my own gaze steadily in the streaky backstage mirror. I hoicked the curve of my bosom into my sequinned corset. My plan was to give myself the perfect lift, one that would later have the audience wondering, *Has she or hasn't she had a boob job?* as I cruised through the bar.

I drew the final arch over my eyebrows, accentuating the wicked gleam that twinkled in my eyes. I was wearing false lashes and crystal jewels, and my lips were smothered with glitter for that perfect "please sir, put it in there" pout.

I mean, what is it that makes someone do what I am about to do? I continued in contemplation.

I could only draw conclusions based on my colourful past, but my answer was this: for most of us it's a combination of things – the need to be seen, to express something we can't express in any other way, to be worshipped with undivided attention. And possibly, in our weaker moments, to seek validation from our peers.

You see, I am a burlesque artiste, an "ecdysiast" if you prefer the more sophisticated term. Or, for the hoi polloi who don't quite grasp the detailed artistry and emotional intelligence of the dance, I'll put it more bluntly:

You could call me … *a stripper*.

Even as I type those words something jars within me. The term is so … crass. Sure, I take my clothes off slowly, writhing around to seductive music. But what I am doing is also something far more complex.

It's cathartic. It's a craft.

It's theatrical. It's therapeutic.

It's healing. It's expressive.

To be quite honest, I think I'd die without it. As, in fact, I nearly have.

If one wants to really understand all the factors that brought me here to this dressing room on Brewer St, Soho in downtown London – miles away from my provincial hometown of Melbourne, Australia, slipping my delicate foot into a royal blue satin stiletto, sliding my hands over my supple legs encased in fishnets, and smoothing double-sided tape onto the back of my newly acquired Agent Provocateur nipple tassels, a seductive gift from a female lover – then one needs to travel with me back in time.

Way, way back. Back to the very first time I felt like this. Back to the very first time I felt her. Back to the very first time I became this creature I am about to become on stage.

Because she is not me. She's someone else.

Ladies and gentlemen, boys and girls, you are about to meet the real author of this book.

Even as I sit here, warmed by the dim flicker of the candle on my desk and the gentle haze of my desk lamp, I can feel her coming on.

She is the one who wants the story to be told.

She is the one who calls the shots.

She is my alter ego, and she has a different name.

Her name is Sapphira.

And she must be obeyed.

It's hard to say what psychological state your mind is in at different times in your life, fundamentally shaping your behaviour. My knowledge of psychology is limited, but I have always been fascinated by Freud's theory of the Id, Ego and Superego and Maslow's Hierachy of Needs. I became aware of these names and philosophies at school, but their principles stuck with me. They resonated deeply with my own experiences of life.

Yes, we are each born with our own unique characters and personalities, but it seems that we are moulded into actors and from an early age, whether we even realise it or not. It is an intricate roleplay. Almost from the minute we are born, we are shaped into acceptable children by well-meaning parents. Our primal urges are slowly tamed and our emotional outbursts are contained. We are shaped as we move into adolescence, and then society at large plays a greater role as we become young, self-conscious adults.

It is my belief at any given moment of the day, in any number of situations or circumstances, we are playing versions of ourselves based on this complex behavioural structuring. We learn very early on what is right and wrong, what is allowed and what is not, what pleases our caregivers, elders, parents, and fundamentally what pleases us. What feels good often becomes a repeated behaviour and eventually a pattern.

What happens, however, when something we find pleasurable evokes the harshest rebuke from our loved ones? Do we favour the safe option and supress that which attracts an angry response, just so we can keep the peace? Surely we can't achieve peace if, in fact, we ourselves are left feeling empty after compromising our own happiness? It is understandably difficult to stand defiant in the face of opposers who condemn the choices we want to make and forbid us from acting upon them.

As I wrote in my opening lines, much of how we behave is a combination of nature – how we are naturally born and programmed to be – and nurture – the repeated programming at the hands of our environment and societal constructs. So how does this relate to my chosen career and my own evolution? What does this mean in the context of my own life, in which I have renamed another side of myself and lived vicariously through her?

Well, it all comes down to the programming I had as a young child.

I sometimes wonder, had I been born into a more liberal family with less rigidity and taboo around sexuality, would I have ever needed to become Sapphira at all? Would I have ever desired an alter ego? Would I have not needed to express myself with a different name? If my experience had been the polar opposite, would I have become "Dorothy" instead, a slipper-loving bookworm who works in a library?

My adult years have led me to believe that that would have not been the case. This energy that is in me – this force, this state of mind, this way of being – would have come to the fore, whether I liked it or not. But perhaps I would have had less shame about stepping into my strong, more dominant self if I had been raised differently. Perhaps I would not have needed to rename that side of myself in order to feel comfortable with it. But the truth is, I am who I am and she is who she is.

Sapphira is my saviour.

I would have died without her, and very nearly did.

My real name is Priscilla Marguerite Silcock and I was born on Tuesday 1st February 1977 to two devoted and deeply caring parents. They wanted nothing more than to support, love and nourish the precious little soul that came into their lives – this warm, pink, crying bundle of joy. I have often quizzed my mother about what time of day I was born and what she remembered about my birth. These are intricate details, some of which she has been unable to answer, because to her all that became inconsequential the moment I appeared in her arms, filling her life with light, hope and a new purpose.

My parents were God-fearing folk and born-again Christians, so reading the Bible and going to our Christian Brethren Church are some of my earliest memories.

My mother was the daughter of Second World War refugees who had fled the refugee camps of Bavaria to find a home on the sunburned shores of Australia's bountiful beauty. My Opa was Hungarian and my Oma was German. My mother was one of four siblings and the second of a pair of twins. I always loved it that my aunty and my mum looked so alike. They are both true natural beauties with sharp cheek bones and slim physiques. They are soft, beautiful, caring people.

My father was born in Portsmouth, England and he met my mother on a trip to Ontario, Canada. They lived together in England for a while, and there they got married before relocating to Melbourne when my father was 28.

We were a humble, working-class family. We've lived in two different houses in Melbourne, Victoria, in that great island known as Australia. My childhood memories are divided distinctly by these two locations, as I was just three years old when we moved to our second bigger home, the back apartment of which I am now living in as I sit here writing.

My fondest memory begins with music; my mother's voice would sing me to sleep. I could feel the vibrations of her throat as I lay warmly encased against her chest. She would stroke my face gently and repeatedly, sending me off to sleep. I know I am small in my earliest recollections, because I see myself standing in a bedroom, the bed towering above me, the boxes of toys under my bed the same height as I am.

It was in that first home I felt something so strong it still stirs within me today. It was the surprise of a gift, a small koala puzzle.

13

I found it wrapped in white tissue paper on my pillow. The overwhelming emotion of happiness and gratitude I felt when I received that koala puzzle is still so vivid, it penetrates through the swirling archive of nostalgia in my mind, forming a crystal-clear moment in time. Considering how few lucid memories I have of that first home, it startles me that this one is so strong. I guess you could call it my first experience of true love.

My mother was, and still is, the most beautiful, self-sacrificing and caring person I have ever met. Being her daughter and having her undivided attention was simply sublime. I revelled in her tender loving care and flourished under her nurturing hands. Her unconditional love is another reason I am here on this planet today. It's the reason I'm able to write this story.

My father was a disciplined and hardworking man. He was sometimes stern and highly intelligent. He was a true fighter and man of principles. I admired his statuesque physical frame, his deep booming voice, and the air of authority with which he carried himself. I sensed he was overwhelmed having two daughters (my sister was born three and half years after I was). Perhaps it was because he was not familiar with the gentle subtlety of the feminine, and he was forced to learn quickly in a house that would soon have a 3:1 female-to-male ratio.

I am so grateful I have my family. In my turbulent, crazy life, in which I have to balance the needs of Sapphira and Priscilla, they have been a constant. Our family home, this place I have recently returned to for a moment of reprieve, has been a solid landing pad. Its strong brick walls are a fortress; its lilting landscape a refuge.

We were a very religious family. My parents had met as born-again Christians and were fervent in their faith and service. Going to church on a Sunday was a way of life for us and our Christian Brethren group was very strict. There are different branches of Christianity like there are different genres of music, and each branch attracts a very distinct set of people and following. Again, this is not dissimilar to music scenes and sub-cultures.

In my early years, I found the Brethren Church overall to be fun and sociable. Sunday School was a place I could be creative, but the main adult assembly meetings seemed very long and boring. I dreaded growing up and having to sit through them. As a youngster I was carefree, able to sit out in the playrooms doing arts and crafts and generally being my joyous, happy self.

The Brethren Church was a place I learnt to love music even more. There was a strong tradition of singing in both Sunday School and the main assembly meetings with the adults. My parents also bought us many sing-a-long reading books with cassette tapes, cementing my love of music. I particularly loved hearing my mother's beautiful, melodious tones soaring above everyone else in the church hall, accompanied by my father's deeper, booming bass notes. There was something about being a group of people, united in voice and resonance, that moved something deeply in all of us. It was profound and indescribable, but I felt it, young as I was. It moved me and it felt bigger than me, bigger than those of us gathered in the room, bigger than everything.

It was thanks to Sunday School that I had my first epiphany.

I was about eight years old and I was invited to sing a song at the close of a theatrical play we were putting on. I chose to sing one of my personal favourites, 'In His Time', a beautiful ballad from one of my favourite Christian songbooks. I remember how nervous I was. The entire room of adults and children sat in a circle around me, a gathering of 20 or so people. As I opened my mouth to sing, I reminded myself to breathe. Suddenly something inside me lit up. My voice, initially timid and quivering, settled into a stronger, more confident stride, and as I progressed I began to feel something magical. It seemed as if the entire room was at a standstill, as if time itself had frozen. There was a palpable current of energy in the air that was both breathtaking and electrifying. I was weightless, drifting in a sea of light and sound. I could not feel my body.

As I reached the final notes of the song, my voice rose in crescendo and the room burst into thunderous applause. Momentarily I had disappeared, but the sharp staccato of applause brought me back into the room with a jolt. I focused and saw many happy, smiling faces.

It was then that I knew.

I knew I wanted to be a singer more than anything in the world. I felt then what would become a theme in my life.

I felt The Pull.

A magnet from another dimension began tugging at my heart. A voice I had always known began calling me. Something inside me opened up and beckoned. Without even knowing I had been asked a question, I said yes. I had found my path, my vocation – or rather it had found me.

Little did I know the turbulent journey that lay ahead of me as I began climbing my Mount Everest.

Unaware of the difficulties I would encounter on the road to self-actualisation, I took a solid first step that day. All I knew is what I felt in my heart. And from that moment, that feeling never left me.

My early years were relatively trouble free. I have a strong sense of love, interspersed with happy memories of my sister being born. I remember the joy of her falling asleep on my chest with her arms around me. It was trusting and intimate. The Brethren Church was a way of life and, like any young child, I accepted life as it was given to me without any knowledge there was even an alternative.

It was when I was around the age of eight that things began to change ...

While Sunday School presented me with the platform to sing, it was also sadly the home of less pleasurable lessons, too. It was at Sunday School where I first learnt to feel sexual shame and inhibition. I learnt about a place called Hell and I learnt about sin. This created a deep sense of uneasiness within my soul. Knowing there was a place of eternal damnation and suffering scared the living daylights out of me. I was worried I would intrinsically be one of those people and that if I was a sinner, I would make God angry enough that he would send me to Hell forever.

While the Brethren Church was a constant theme in my childhood, there was something else that profoundly shaped my early belief systems. It is the book upon which the Brethren Church is based. To some it's known as the Scriptures; to others it's the Good Book, but to most of us it has one familiar title. It is the Bible.

A wonderfully rich source of lessons, philosophies and even erotic literature, the Bible was a book I would grow to know intimately, and more intimately than most, given that I was raised in a devoutly fervent Brethren family.

The Bible is divided into two sections: the Old Testament and the New Testament. In Sunday School we would learn the key stories from the Bible in various ways, including reading books, drawing, making paper cut-outs, listening to stories and, of course, re-enacting parts of it in the much-anticipated Sunday School Play.

Reflecting back on the premise that we are involuntarily governed by both elements of nature and nurture, I realise that something else was very evident in my personality from the beginning. The ancient Greeks called her Aphrodite. She is one of the seven female Goddess archetypes – the lover and seductress. Indeed, her presence in me was tangible. I was innocent and unaware, but my own sensual powers dwelt strongly within me, as did my ability to express that side of myself through movement. This would prove to be a controversial theme throughout my life, but it all began at the Sunday School Play.

I was a true-born thespian, and the Sunday School Play was my first encounter with the theatre. There was a stage manager (Mrs No Nonsense), a set designer (my dad), a wardrobe department (my mum), a prop maker (my Dad), a director and choreographer (Mrs No Nonsense), and promoters (my mum and dad). It didn't matter to me that we were only in a dingy church hall; this was a stage and I got to be on it. I was in heaven. (I hadn't even heard of my favourite stage light called the "follow spot" back then. Oh, the Sunday School Play I could put on now!)

Nonetheless, armed with this small-scale crew, I knew I was about to make a grand entrance and I would give it my all.

Our first Sunday School production was the famous story of Daniel and the Lions' Den. I could summarise it briefly for you here but really you don't need to worry about the plot. The main thing you need to know is to look out for me on the stage. That's really all you need to know ever, so as long as you know that, we'll get on just fine!

This play would be my first experience of being what I know now to be a chorus line dancer. That's right, my first part was in fact one of the lions in Daniel's den, the ring-leader in a pack of man-eating lions. (One defenceless male was our sole target – whoever would have thought!)

The music for our play was from an American Christian music production team. They had created a slick series of songs and backing tracks, and I loved the groovy music we got to dance to as the lions. We even had leotards and little swinging tails to wear around our waists.

After a few weeks of rehearsal, the big night rolled around.

I donned my tail along with my fellow dancers and waited nervously for my chance to "go on" – a phrase I would hear many times in later years as my career progressed in show business.

As the story moved forward, it came around to our part of the performance. Accompanied by my fellow lions, I made my entrance. Something similar to my first singing experience happened – I switched on!

A light bulb was switched on and I came alive. I swung my hips and wriggled my tail. I felt one with the music and the rhythm; the joy of dancing for an audience left me energised and alive. We pounced around with feline movements, our tails swooshing in time. As the number drew to a close, we fell into our final position and posed.

Like the first time I had sung, I felt a jolt of electricity. It felt great.

Unlike the first time, the applause was reserved.

We left the stage on cloud nine, the satisfying post-show adrenaline coursing through our veins. Yet there was something about this performance that was different. Something had changed.

Later that night as we drove home in car, my father announced that there had been some disapproval among the Brothers, the men of our Christian Brethren community. He went on to explain that at future Sunday Schools there was to be no music on a sound system and that they would only use piano music instead. There would also be no dancing, no leotards and no costumes.

There was something between his words that carried a heavier meaning, a sharper disapproval. A foreboding and ominous air descended over the car. It was impenetrable, unmoving and formidable. I was frightened.

I could not quite read the context of the situation. There was a cryptic message in his tone and an unspoken condemnation. I knew I had done something very, very wrong.

I panicked. I could not understand what I had done that was so bad. I was even more dumbfounded because it had felt fantastic!

A deep sense of grief set in. I lost something valuable that day, something I was too young to articulate. But it was a lesson I took into my soul. Dancing with carefree abandon was dangerous and could get me into a lot of trouble. I was worried I had upset God. I knew that he didn't like people who sinned, and I felt sure this reaction and unspoken shame from my father meant I had committed a big sin, even bigger than taking an extra cookie from the cookie tin when no one was looking at church morning tea.

Then my grief turned into anger.

I was angry at Mrs No Nonsense, angry at Sunday School, and angry at myself. Deep down I was angry at God too.

That impenetrable and foreboding reaction from my father would become more and more familiar to me as I grew into adolescence. It was not long after this that I endured another traumatic scene that still dwells deep inside the recesses of my mind. I was very little and had few possessions I truly prized, but music was one thing that brought me untold, limitless joy. I had a set of favourite cassettes and records and I would listen to them over and over. But one afternoon a bizarre and disturbing incident occurred. I walked into the backyard of our home to find a bonfire burning and my father standing over it. The flames were frightening and the acrid smell even more so, singeing the hair in my nostrils, burning all the way down into the back of my throat ...

As I got closer to the fire, I was shocked to see a pile of music, cassette tapes and records in my father's hands.

In an eerie cleansing ritual, this fervent and protective man was burning all the non-Christian music in the house.

He meant well – he wanted our home to be pure and for all our music to honour God – but I was devastated. Music was the one thing I loved and yet even my *Oliver Twist* record was in the pile of condemned materials. I begged and pleaded for the record not to be burnt, but my pleas fell on deaf ears. Along with Cliff

Richard, Barry Manilow and many other harmless composers, my *Oliver Twist* record was thrown on the pile and engulfed in a ball of flames.

I lost something again that day. Something personal and private began to shut down within me. More so, I made an unconscious association with men and music: men were untrustworthy with it. This mistrust would later wreak havoc in my professional career as a singer / songwriter, as most collaboration is with males. I was scarred, and it tarnished many future interactions in the recording studio and in the music industry at large.

Sundays were not all doom and gloom, though, as some music was still allowed in my life. One favourite Sunday tradition, when we did not stay at church for the later afternoon meeting, was watching reruns of old musicals on TV. My mother was more lenient at home and loved music. It was my father who was stricter.

I adored all the musicals we watched. I loved Julie Andrews, Shirley Temple, Perry Mason, and Marilyn Monroe. Rogers and Hammerstein musicals delighted me. I revelled in the grand costumes and opulent sets, the phenomenal choreographed dance routines. I would close my eyes and picture myself on the set, one of the glamorous women. I saw myself with my eyes closed, head tilted back, being kissed by Prince Charming.

I admired the tongue-in-cheek way that female sensuality was presented. It was done with such class. It was shown in the cut of a costume, the flash of a leg or an elegant gloved hand. I could drink it in for hours and I revelled in the fantasy and escapism of this bygone era. The modern-day fashions left so much to be desired in my eyes. I longed for a revival of that moment in time. The glamour and sophistication were unsurpassable.

Music ran in our family. My English grandfather loved jazz music and had been teaching himself to play piano. He died before I got to meet him. My mother was also a singer who had been in a trio act; she'd had some professional work as a young woman. She had a beautiful voice and her love of music was so strong that she had paid for her own piano lessons as a teenager out of her own pocket money.

To this day I love rifling through the hundreds of pieces of sheet music she bought. Thankfully these somehow escaped the bonfire cleansing ritual, and they truly captured a musical moment in time. They included Dusty Springfield, *Carousel*, and The Mamas and The Papas.

I also still had music in my life in the form of the piano, which I had started to play when I was only five years old. Because my mother always felt that she had started to learn an instrument too late in life, she was determined to provide a source of encouragement and discipline with our music lessons, the kind of support she had lacked from her own parents.

The first time I found myself sitting in front of a piano, I was entranced by the black and white keys and the sounds they made when I pushed on them with my finger. My tiny frame was dwarfed by this enormous feat of musical engineering, my small fingers barely reaching four notes apart. A sheet of music was placed in front of me, the squiggly black shapes seeming as legible as Egyptian hieroglyphics. Yet somehow I was meant to learn what they all meant, and to create sounds from them on this gigantic wooden soundbox

The whole process of learning an instrument was truly daunting. Miss Melancholy – my first piano teacher who always seemed to have a vacant stare to match her sparsely furnished home – was also quite scary. But my mother was determined we would learn to play piano, and thus my foray into music began.

Every day she would make sure we did our piano exercises, and it became part of family life and routine.

I frequently rebelled about the rigidity of daily practice, feigning illness regularly. But I soon learnt that there was no compromise, and secretly I was enjoying learning to play.

When I was seven years old my mother started taking me to ballet classes. The Ballet School was a delightful little studio run by Miss Ballerina. It was a tiny brick building nestled on a grassy nature strip on the main road opposite the local town hall. I liked wearing ballet slippers and leotards. Learning to dance was glorious fun, and for the first time I was put on stage outside of something involved with the Sunday School Play. It was good for my soul.

'First position, then second ... lift, girls, lift!' Miss Ballerina would call to us encouragingly. In that small, mirrored ballet studio, I would learn to plié. I learnt the various ballet positions of the feet and practised dance exercises at the barre.

Yet again, I had the chance to be in a stage production and the baby showgirl in me was jigging with delight.

Ballet lessons brought something else to my world. A deepening love of music was forming. This time my ears were introduced to the beauty of classic orchestral symphonies. For this introduction I owe Miss Ballerina a debt of gratitude.

Our first ballet performance was to *Morning, Peer Gynt* by De Grieg. The haunting swell of strings stirred emotions deeply in me and I was once again swept off my feet. I heard the instruments playing in this glorious composition and it sounded as they though they had their own language and were talking to each other. I wanted to understand what they were saying, and somewhere deep inside me I felt I understood, even though there were no words being exchanged. In this quiet repose and solitude I once again felt something bigger than me and bigger than all of us. I was awestruck.

CHAPTER 2

POISON

'I am come into my garden ...
I have gathered my myrrh with my spice ...'

Song of Solomon 5:1

It is the greatest gift to be born in this physical form and to mature each year. As a child I found it rewarding to become more adept at tasks. Tying my own shoelaces was a huge triumph; so was gaining a pen licence at school. And oh, the sweet joy of developing as a musician! I have found the process of ageing to be a fascinating experience, as if I am the co-pilot of a mystical vessel that has, in some ways, a predetermined path.

My own body flourished, and the dexterity of my hands improved as I drilled piano scales and exercises each day as a child. I became a less self-conscious pianist and Miss Melancholy wooed me away from "cheating" – developing musical skills by ear, listening to her play the example of the piece, then mimicking it back. Rather than reading the notes of music, I watched her fingers and used my auditory comprehension to translate the melody. But to be a true musician, it was thought to be better if I could decipher those squiggly Egyptian-like hieroglyphics and read the actual notes.

Initially, and to her credit, Miss Melancholy suggested I was showing a predisposition to learn music via a new formula called the Suzuki Method. This method was based on the concept that a child can learn to speak their native spoken language naturally, and so it should be with music. To this day, I have always regretted not being encouraged in this style. Gradually I became totally dependent on sheet music being in front of me, in order to be able to play anything at all. (Imagine only feeling confident to speak what you can read from a page.) It was a very unnatural way to bond with the piano, and some 30 years later I envy jazz and self-taught musos who are at one with their instruments, able to play as easily and freely as they can speak the spoken word.

Thus, the wrestle began. I had to master not only reading and writing the alphabet at school, but the additional ability to read music and make my pudgy fingers hit the right black and white keys. I wonder if Mozart faced this conundrum?

The daily rituals of Christian Brethren life and the discipline of piano playing became the norm. Well, it was normal for me. But soon I began to realise how unlike other families we were. School exposed me to other children from all walks of life, and it seemed to me that I was getting a raw deal. Other kids got to watch all the TV they wanted. They even had the telly on at breakfast and through mealtimes. They stayed up as late as they wanted to, had teenage magazines and got to have junk food like white bread and soft drinks.

This brings me to the greatest tribulation that interfered with my overall wellbeing and perception of normality: the Christian Brethren community.

As I described earlier, there are very many different branches of religion, and even within the overarching umbrella of Christianity there are smaller divisions, rather like one might see on an organisational structure, organogram or flow chart. Christianity is an extremely broad term that branches off into multiple offshoots of smaller organisations. There are the Baptists, the Pentecostals, the Presbyterians, and the Methodists. Even the Brethren division itself has sub-sects. I soon learnt that our group was particularly strict, rigid and quite condemning of any other practice. While I was a youngster I had no concept of the damage that a group of people held in high esteem – even as elders and role models – could do to a young, impressionable mind. I have since learnt that the Brethren have been widely condemned in the media and labelled a cult. While I do not think of myself as a cult survivor, I have been able to see – with the insight and broader perception afforded to me from life experience – how much of my distress stemmed from living among this narrow-minded minority.

In most group dynamics I feel I have been somewhat of a misfit. I have been too flamboyant, too outspoken, too gregarious, too theatrical. 'Oh Priscilla,' my mother would exclaim in exasperation. 'You're just too much!'

I would try so hard to tone myself down, to rein in this effervescing life force and energy that seemed to pour, involuntarily, out of my every cell. I just loved life, and I threw myself into every activity wholeheartedly. If I was doing something at all, I was giving it my all. My all seemed to be about 100% more than everyone else's.

'I just don't know how you do it all.' People have said this to me all my life. Perhaps learning piano as well as being enrolled full-time at school meant that from a very early age I was used to working extracurricular hours. I was used to having two disciplines, two careers, two lives. This is just who I am, and even now I am constantly trying to keep myself in check. As I have matured, I have also realised that much of this boundless energy and infectious enthusiasm is an incredible gift. I have leadership traits, ones which I'm very proud to possess.

*

Our Christian Brethren Church was the first place I felt out of place. The rules and regimes were frightening and weird. The menfolk had total dominance, and Mr Condemnation was one of the leading elderly Brothers. At Sunday meetings or even in our homes at Bible study, women such as me, my mother, and Mrs No Nonsense had to have our heads covered with a scarf. We were not permitted to speak, preach, or teach within the walls of the church hall. Thankfully, we were allowed to sing, and this was one of the saving graces of those long Sundays. I would relish joining in in some of the powerful hymns. The soaring voices, including my own, would lift me to higher places. I was always tuning into my mother's voice. She had the most natural tone, and even in her upper register she would reach each note with ease and grace. My voice was undeveloped, and it frustrated me. The higher up the scale I got the more it would hurt my throat. Sometimes I would even leave the Sunday meetings feeling hoarse from the strain. It was as if my voice was stuck. I would reach a certain point and almost choke with the constriction of muscles and air. It was a vast and impassable obstacle, and it was like trying to climb over a gate.

'How you do sing, Mummy?' I would quiz her. 'How can I sing up high like you?'

She would hold my hand with her warm touch and explain that it was all to do with the breath. She told me that one day, when I was old enough, I should also try singing lessons. I was really quite in awe of her voice and her beauty. Those dulcet vibrations resonated deep into my core. Sitting on her lap or standing next to her when we sang hymns was the ecstasy of my otherwise dreaded Sundays.

We were not allowed to have an accompaniment in the main meetings. We sang only a cappella, and not in the vibrant, joyous way you would think of a Gospel choir. It was sombre, prolonged; a mournful set of hymns that dragged on and on. It seemed to me like they had been written in the dinosaur ages.

Mr Condemnation, however, seemed to be in his element. He would stand and boom reproachful messages and interpretations of the Scriptures. The wording of those parts of the Bible with which he had such an affinity were so old fashioned, I wondered if Mr Condemnation had been preserved a fossil – perhaps he was as ancient as the pages these words came from. He was certainly wrinkly and hairless enough; that comb-over wasn't fooling anyone, not even my untrained show producer's eye! I would get Hair and Make-Up onto him stat if he was going to make an appearance in my production.

Another unhealthy habit began with this Sunday regime. My mother had been very watchful over our diets, and we were not allowed many sugary treats. And yet, on Sundays, there would be a morning tea break, during which a cupboard filled with huge packets of biscuits would be opened. My parents were often distracted during this part of the morning. I don't know if it was rebellion or anxiety, but I developed the habit of shoving handfuls of biscuits into my pockets and taking them to the toilets to eat. I would stuff them into my mouth behind the cubicle door. It was calming to fill my stomach with rich, sugary biscuits. It also became a ritual at my Oma's house, where there were also bountiful tins of biscuits. Each time it was the same: I would wait until no one was looking, grab a huge handful of whatever I could get my hands on, and retreat to the toilet where I would be left uninterrupted. This binge eating was frenzied and unnatural, but it was a way to get my own back and also, somehow, to feel safe. The behaviour plagues me to this day – I can always tell that my emotional state is under duress if I find myself heading to the corner shop or vending machine for a chocolate fix!

At the Brethren Church, the main Breaking of Bread meetings were steeped in tradition. I would learn later in life that it all began with a different sect of the Brethren Church, the Plymouth Brethren, originating from England. Our particular Christian Assembly group was, in actual fact, not as strict as others. There was an even more fervent community I was aware of in our area called the Exclusive Brethren and they were totally shut off from the real world. Most of the children were home schooled; they were not allowed to dine with Non-Believers. In the Exclusive

Brethren, the womenfolk had to have their heads covered at all times, even while out in public. The dowdiness of their ankle-length skirts and long, straight hair (which they were not allowed to cut) was an eye-sore. I shudder to think what that upbringing would have been like in comparison to my minutely less orthodox experience.

On the other side of the scale was the Open Brethren. I never got to associate with that lot. Even having the word "open" in their name makes me warm to them. They had open worship, and anyone could join their meetings. Personally, I think I would have thrived in something groovy like an up-tempo Baptist church. A girl I met at school went there, and they had a rock band play at all their sermons. They had a vibrant youth group who went to the cinema or bowling; they didn't just gather in a circle to study the Bible ad nauseam like we did at youth meetings.

I was always devilishly trying to spice up the boredom of our youth events. I once managed to tie Mr Condemnation's shoelaces together, and the entire youth group hooted riotously when he took his first step and came crashing down onto a pile of bean bags! Thankfully, no one got in trouble for this since, despite their dryness, the crowd were still up for a good laugh.

In all sects of Brethren there were some rules that were always adhered to. Only the Brothers, the men of the Brethren Church, could talk out loud and address the group with sermons. We had a Breaking of the Bread ritual in the main Sunday meeting, where a loaf of bread – symbolising the body of Christ – and a glass of wine, symbolising His blood, was passed among the group. Only those who had been assessed as being true Believers and part of the local Christian Brethren Assembly were permitted to partake, and youngsters were not involved until they reached a certain coming of age. Outsiders or even Christian Brethren from other congregations could join, as long as they first had a Letter of Commendation sent ahead of them to Brothers of the local group they planned to attend. It was a very complex dynamic, and there was always an undertone of condemnation – or, at worst, the threat of being outcast – if ever you were found to be wilfully sinning or breaking any of the principles for Christian Brethren living.

The key message for acceptance in our Christian Brethren community was accepting Christ as your saviour and, in doing this, committing to living a life without sin. You also had to repent as soon as you noticed you may have sinned. It was expected of me to accept Christ as my saviour from an early age, and I knew this.

Of course, I would want to be saved. My parents had accepted Christ as their saviour and they were going to Heaven when they died, so if I didn't accept Christ as my saviour, we would be separated. Even worse, I would go to Hell, which I learnt was a place of "gnashing of teeth and eternal damnation".

The other concept I was taught at church was very heavy for youngsters to comprehend, but somehow my artistic, intelligent mind understood it. The concept was that the rest of the world of Non-Believers was condemned, and there would be something called The Rapture. Here Christ would come to take all the Believers with him. We had to be ready at any given minute.

I remember the haunting lyrics of a song we used to sing called 'I Wish We'd All Been Ready'. It spoke of two people asleep in bed; one hears a noise and turns their head to find the second person gone. In another verse, two people are walking up a hill and are separated at this same, precise moment. One of them, the Believer, disappears and is whisked safely to Heaven. The other, the Non-Believer, is left standing alone on Earth, which is about to be condemned to flames. The chorus of the song was set to a sombre minor melody and warned that you, too, would be left behind if you didn't change your mind and repent. We sang it repeatedly at church. It was almost a brainwashing exercise.

There was no warning about The Rapture, also called the Second Coming of Christ. This could happen at any minute and I was petrified.

I vividly remember waking to a deathly quiet house some nights and leaping out of bed in a panic, tearing around the house to see if The Rapture had happened. I feared it deeply in my heart of hearts. I had not made the cut and was now left behind to burn, to be engulfed in the fiery flames that would punish a woe-begone sinner like me.

I felt sure I would be punished.

I felt, somehow, that I was unforgivable.

And I deserved it.

In the midst of all this confusion, I was beginning some tentative artist exploration. My piano skills were developing enough that I could sit and tinker with just the very basic notes on one hand. This instrument turned into my life-saver; it gave me a different way to express myself that words could not. I felt my heart leap and soar when I played certain combinations of notes and chords.

Every   Good   Boy   Deserves   Fruit

This rhyme helped me to learn the position of notes on a stave. Even I surprised myself as slowly my hands began placing themselves in the right place at the right time. I could play each note in time without needing to concentrate quite so hard. I was enjoying this moment of unconscious competence. I was reaching this effortless ability of producing sounds on the piano.

The Brethren Church had a pianist and piano accordion player called Miss Sensible. I quite like the analogy that people pick pets who look like themselves, and I think it's the same with instruments. They are an encapsulation of that person's essence.

I had a natural affinity for the piano, and I revelled in the sensuous engagement of the fingers, using the touch of both hands and multiple fingers to play multiple polyphonic sounds. The voice, too, was a fitting instrument for me: the use of the tongue, breath and vibration fitted me perfectly. They are such intimate elements of the core of expression, and they are linked in many ways to sexuality.

In a similar way, Miss Sensible was inclined towards the portly girth of the piano accordion. A somewhat out-dated musical endeavour, it suited her to a T. She would hoist this cumbersome device over both shoulders to cover her bosoms. (In truth, any covering of womanly curves was applauded in the Brethren Church. I wonder how they would have reacted to a cellist or harpist with her legs spread wide apart?) Miss Sensible would then push and heave the piano accordion's pleated bellow across her equally portly abdomen, producing a wondrous funfair carnival sound. I liked hearing her play immensely, and occasionally she would let me try to play the keys which looked similar to those on the piano. But there was so much else to learn on the piano accordion, with the pumping and heaving. I could never produce the sound I desired, so I decided to stick with the humble upright, with which at last I was beginning to show some familiarity.

Thus it was that when I was around the age of 11, a truly astonishing thing occurred. Well, two truly astonishing things.

As I found myself sitting alone during a bout of piano practice at home – during which I was desperately struggling to find focus – I let my hands wander idly over the piano keys.

Delicately licking at each ivory key, my mind also wandered. I felt as if in a daze when suddenly I found myself playing a repeated loop. A tune began to emerge … and as it emerged some words came with it.

Lo and behold, I had started writing my first song!

We had started a world project at school, and I had also been participating in the 40 Hour Famine arranged by World Vision. It was a charity event where people sponsored you to go without food to raise money for people living in countries with little or no supplies to feed themselves. I was young, but not so young that I couldn't see the injustice of the wasted food I saw in my world. It was such a contrast to the starving faces I would see on the posters of 40 Hour Famine advertisement. How could these communities be struggling for food when we threw so much out?

The world that we are living in

Is a pretty big one

So we all need to join together

So we can all sing a happy song

There are people who are wondering what

The day is gonna bring

There are people who are starving

What kind of good song can they sing?

CHORUS:

Change the world

Change the world

We've got to change the world

So that everyone feels equal and the same

Change the world

Change the world

We've got to change the world

Oh we've got to change the world

I wrote this down, frantically scribbling words. I then started playing again, my pencil wedged between my teeth as my hands moved deftly over the keys.

I felt it again.

I felt The Pull.

I knew I wanted to do this!

Just as the words of my song were forming, I knew I wanted to change the world with music. I was beginning to see the path for my dream ... It was hazy and a bit foggy, but in the recesses of my mind a plan was beginning to take shape.

I was exploring as an artist.

I was also exploring my body.

At about the same time, I was discovering something else. I had begun exploring my body, and I found something that felt good. I knew it was private and I found a place I liked to touch. It was a place down below, and I would only touch it down under the covers of my bed. It was somewhere private, but it felt good and it relaxed me. I knew I shouldn't let anyone else catch me doing it, so I would only do it in private – in bed, or the bath, or in the dark. I didn't stop to think whether it was a sin or not, because it was something I discovered naturally, and it felt lovely.

I started to repeat this activity more and more, and sometimes if I had trouble sleeping it would help me to get to sleep. One day, when I thought I was alone in my room, I closed my eyes. I was in this warm, hazy feeling when suddenly a voice jolted me back to reality.

'Priscilla, what are you doing?!' My mother's shriek pierced the silence and shattered my reverie. Tearing the sheets back, she found me exposed and ashamed. I leapt up. Her face bore a twisted expression I had never seen before. 'Stop that immediately!' she said.

I could not meet her gaze. I did not know what to say.

But I lost something again that day. My coin was tarnished. My light was snuffed out.

CHAPTER 3

TAKE ME TO THE HOSPITAL

'In the shadows
He is hiding
In the darkness
Alone, abiding'
Sapphira's song to DJ Shadow

It became such a struggle to be myself. It seemed easier to pretend to be the person my parents wanted me to be. It was not just my mother and father's approval I desperately wanted to win. So, too, I sought the approval of the Christian Brethren community, for I was nearing the Age of Understanding. It would soon be expected of me to be baptised and to commence the Breaking of the Bread ceremony. My days of spending time outside the main meetings on Sundays where I could be creative, read stories, draw and play children's games was nearing an end. I was reaching adolescence and getting ready to start high school. The transition from primary school to high school seemed a terrifying prospect, and I was fraught with more anxiety than most. I also knew I was reaching the age where my commitment at church would increase, with more pressure to be the best Christian and representative of Christ I could be. If I could live an exemplary life and share the Bible with people as often as possible, I might achieve more favour and praise by converting a Non-Believer.

At our youth groups we were encouraged to come up with tactics and ways to "witness" out in our local community, to save the lost souls of others who were condemned to die in the fiery flames of Hell for eternity. The onus was on us. We were the Saved, the Believers. We had a duty to help rescue others, too. I was reaching this internal crisis and the only way I could see fit was to be two versions of myself. At high school, among my new-found friends and peers, I wanted to fit in. I would swear, eventually smoke cigarettes and read "worldly" magazines. Then, at home, I would switch into the most devout and pristine Christian imaginable. I would dutifully read my Bible and say my prayers. Every Sunday I prayed to Jesus to forgive my hypocrisy as I opened my mouth to eat his flesh and sipped the salty wine of his blood. These morsels entered my lips laden with the worst kind of poison. I was ingesting my own failure, my own hypocrisy. My very existence and natural inclinations were so repulsive that they would surely lead to my death. Each sour mouthful would course over my teeth and flick around my tongue like grit. It would turn into the grimiest sludge, sliding down the back of my throat and gagging me with guilt. I was disgusted with myself for living the lie, for being the accursed "Sunday Christian" we were warned never to become.

I didn't know if could be forgiven. In fact, I was pretty sure I couldn't be, because it was said to me repeatedly that your sins would be not be forgiven if you committed them wilfully.

I knew God could see everything, and even though I could hide from my parents behind a thin veil of pretence, there was no hiding from His all-seeing eye. In the Bible there were countless examples of people who had tried to deceive His omnipotent self and they came to an untimely demise. God could strike at any moment, with the harshest punishment for wilful sinners. Lot's wife was turned to a pillar of salt; Ananias and Sapphira stole from God and He killed them. I was sure I was in this same classification of unredeemable outcasts.

I began to spend my days waiting for God to kill me.

I wondered why the human race even existed. Why did He create us if He knew most of us would not choose the right path, if He knew we would wind up tortured and tormented in a place of indescribable, unimaginable suffering for all eternity?

What kind of twisted, all-knowing super power chose to bring people to life, give them these amazing sexual sensations in their bodies and then damn them forevermore if they could not resist their own impulses?

None of it made sense. And I when I dared to even ask the Christian Brethren youth group and elders these kinds of questions, I was always told that God creates us to have free choice, and it is in fact we who choose that horrific place of Hell.

It seemed that anything fun, enjoyable, and interesting was a sin. I was damned if I did commit to Christ and live the life of a faultless Believer, and I was damned if I didn't, because another fear drilled into me was the theory that Christianity would be banned as The Rapture came closer. The inevitable test for the devoutness of our faith would come to pass when we would be tortured at the hands of the Secret Police and Government for our beliefs.

One day at a Sunday School camp, we were shown a horrific video of Christians being tortured. Their fingernails were going to be pulled from their hands with forceps. The camera closed in menacingly on a trembling finger. I ran out of the room. Even while writing these words now, my heart leaps with panic as I think of that image.

I was in such despair, such conflict. This weighed on my mind day and night, night and day. The only place I had to retreat to was the solace and refuge of my piano.

By now I was becoming a much more competent pianist. I would while away the hours at the keys, sometimes learning sheet music, sometimes playing scales, and other times just letting those sweet wooden vibrations seep soothingly into my soul. The piano and I were one and music was my saviour. All that confusion – all my guilt, remorse, shame, conflict, fear, joy, and despair – poured into melodies. I began writing prolifically. It was as if the music healed me. Each note anchored me, reassured me, and wrapped me up in a safe and caring blanket of sound.

My parents were deeply loving and thoughtful towards me. My father was a great handyman and could fix anything you put before him. I loved watching him tinker under the car or mow the lawn. He would often let me help with chores and we would have moments of real father – daughter bonding doing those activities. My mother was the most self-sacrificing and thoughtful soul I knew; she was forever baking a cake for this or that person, writing cards, delivering bunches of flowers, and looking after elderly people in the street by popping in for a visit. She was a real bundle of energy and laughter, too. She often wrote the sweetest notes and put them in my socks or lunch boxes. I've kept a whole shoebox full of notes from her over the years; they always made my heart leap with joy.

There is no denying that they were doting and loving parents who wanted the absolute best for me. They worked hard to provide for my every need. I adored both of them with my whole being for the love they showed me. That's why it was so much harder to stand up for the life I wanted to have, for the person I really wanted to be. How could I ever tell them I didn't want or believe in Christianity? How could I tell them that I would choose the Non-Believer's life, which would mean eventual damnation in Hell?

The longer I spent time at high school the more I realised there were alternative ways of living and much more liberal parents, families and lifestyles. And it was in high school that I really became interested in boys. With all those hormones wreaking havoc in my body, I was noticing changes as I grew breasts and pubic hair. But above all, I had developed some serious crushes on the opposite sex at school.

I went to a coeducational school that specialised in music. It was outside our immediate school zoning area, so we had to apply specially to be granted enrolment. My application showed my now extensive music repertoire, as I had completed Grade 5 Australian Music Examination Board level and a level of music theory, too. All these papers were photocopied and posted in an envelope along with my enrolment form. There was a celebration in our family when I was first accepted, and then later my sister. Being at one of the state's finest music schools was pretty much one of the best things that ever happened to me, and I am thankful that my father could see the benefit in enhancing my musical ability, despite knowing the curriculum would focus on the classics and light pop music. I was relieved that his attitudes towards secular music had relaxed since the bonfire incident; he had loved Carole King, The Animals, and pop bands likes Hermin's Hermits before becoming a born-again Christian!

At last I met lots of other diligent geeks who, like me, would wake early to practise their instruments or take lunch breaks to rehearse. And, above all, there was band camp!

I was now being exposed to music of all genres, as well as people from all walks of life. Our school had a huge reputation in the music world, and we had multiple award-winning groups such as the orchestra, jazz, choir, and stage band. I loved the sound of the professional stage band and orchestra. I would sing in the choir and later conduct our House group.

It was reaffirmed to me again: music evoked something in me.

Every hair on my neck would stand on end.

What was happening was bigger than me, bigger than all of us.

Bigger than everything.

As I was already very proficient with piano and continuing private education outside school, it was suggested I should learn the French horn as my second instrument. My choices of harp or guitar were not available. I wasn't sure about this cumbersome and heavy instrument; I tentatively suggested I would prefer then to learn the sax which had a sassy, sexy feel. But the teachers advised me that if I wanted to audition for music school it would be better to be proficient in a rarer instrument like the French horn because sax, voice and piano were very popular and fiercely competitive. As the French horn was more unusual, it would be easier to gain acceptance into the best music schools, and then I could switch to the instrument of my choice.

I was so used to people telling me what to do and agreeing with it that I acquiesced. I lived to regret it every day of my life for the next four years, because it turned out I absolutely hated everything about that darn French horn.

At school I experienced my first kiss, and in true Priscilla style it was an event of monumental proportions.

Imagine 50 hyperactive teenagers. Imagine that those 50 teenagers are very extroverted, all of them musicians. Now imagine sending them away for a week to a residential, coeducational camp. I think you're starting to get the picture ...

It was a hotbed of sexual attraction and flirtation.

I seemed to catch the eye of Mr Handsome, who was two years (two years!) older than me. In high-school terms, that is dating way out of your league. I was so smitten with this guy that I used to write his name in a love heart in my diary and daydream about him with all the innocence that teenage lust affords one. I could not believe it when at band camp he seemed to catch my eye. I puffed and wheezed in frustration at the mouthpiece of my French horn, wishing the earth would swallow me whole as he casually slid his hand up and down the length of his trumpet, producing a comfortably suave toot. My face, which was already red with exertion, burnt crimson with embarrassment as he held my gaze for an invitingly long moment in time.

As rehearsal came to an end, he came to speak to me and suggested I should come to the boys' dorm at midnight when all the teachers would be asleep.

I knew we had been strictly forbidden to cross the hallway that divided the boys' from the girls' sides of the room. But this was Mr Handsome, and invitations like this would not come around again!

I didn't hesitate to agree, and with all the angst of young lust I was on cloud nine, counting down the hours until bedtime.

As it neared midnight my dorm was abuzz with activity. Each dorm had six beds, and all the girls in mine knew I was going to make a break for it and trespass into the forbidden domain. There were words of caution and encouragement from the other five bunks near my bed. As with most of my major life events, this was causing a divide. Some of the girls were worried I'd get caught and get us all in trouble, others were egging me on because it was so daring, and they were enjoying the thrill of it without having to take the risk themselves. It was just a little tête-à-tête, but what's a kiss without some controversy, I ask you?

I enquired among the group if they had suggestions about how to French kiss, as this meant using your tongue. As Mr Handsome was two years older, I was pretty sure he would expect a French kiss and I had never done it before. So here we were, six girls in my dorm, practising on the curve of our arms inside our elbows. I wasn't sure this drill gave me any more experience or confidence, but I was glad I at least practised. I was a pianist, and practice, as they say, makes perfect! The next issue was to not have bad breath.

One of my dorm mates offered mints, but I declined. To be absolutely sure my mouth tasted alright, I decided to eat half a tube of toothpaste instead. It tasted disgusting and almost made me vomit, but I managed to wash it down with water.

At last midnight rolled around. It was showtime.

I crept with stealth out of our dorm and glided, in socks, along the corridor. Crossing the landing between the two wings – divided by a huge staircase – was a cinch. Before I knew it, I was in the boys' dorm, actually clambering up the ladder to the top bunk where Mr Handsome was waiting. I said a brief hello to all the other boys in the dorm. It doesn't surprise me now that even that first foray into intimacy also included an audience! I'm not sure what they were all thinking as Mr Handsome and I sidled closer to each other under his doona (duvet) in the bunk bed.

There was little time for conversation. I was more focused on getting the task at hand out of the way. So, I reached forward, pointing my head in the general direction of his. I was open mouthed and began lapping with my tongue in the way I'd practised moments earlier on my arm. For a few minutes it seemed to be going well, until he pulled back and said 'Um … I'm really sorry, but that's my nose!'

I was mortified! In the dark, in my anxiety, I had missed his mouth and was giving heartfelt, tender French kisses to the inside of his nostrils! No wonder it felt wet.

I recoiled in total shock. I was stunned and frozen, but this was only temporary. Quickly enough I shot bolt upright and scaled out of the door. My movements were less cautious this time as I clambered back outside and thumped across the landing. But alas, who should I see coming up the stairs but our head music teacher, Miss Policy! Miss Policy took one look at me and could see I was leaving the boys' dormitory. I was nowhere near the girls' side. She accosted me, grabbing my arm curtly. In a few short minutes my parents had been called. It was 2am.

Yes, that's right. My parents came to collect me at 9am that next morning – and it was Sunday, church day.

I had to do the most shameful walks of shame, and was marched into the Christian Brethren church hall right in time for the morning meeting. I was dead sure everyone knew of my escapade; gossip travelled fast in that tight-knit group of do-gooders. I couldn't meet anyone's eye as I recoiled in shame. There was quite a level of hilarity even inside me, though, as inside I was laughing about the whole situation. But, on a more sinister note, my humour was short-lived because I was pretty sure it was God who had sent Miss Policy across my path. This was His small warning about not sinning beneath His all-seeing gaze.

Worldly music was frowned upon in the Christian Brethren, but as my high-school years went past and I was studying at one of the most renowned music schools, I began to be introduced to more and more styles of music and from all eras. English class was a treasured hour and I loved both my English and English Literature teachers equally. We were exploring more provocative texts and, as I was a budding lyricist, I was taking note of the burgeoning cultural rebellion. The 80s saw hip hop rise to the fore, along with heavy metal and rock bands.

Enter boyfriend number two: Mr Metal. A guitarist with the signature long hair of the heavy metal scene, Mr Metal was both financially more established – with a regular part-time job – and artistically thrilling for me. I knew he was also sexually experienced because it was something us girls discussed among ourselves. I found all of these traits highly alluring, and soon I was regularly visiting his home. The walls of his room were adorned with posters of his idols: Iron Maiden, Korn, Fear Factory and James Hetfield from Metallica. I liked the sound of heavy metal and I liked the defiance of the lyrics, the anger, the power. The occasional lilting ballads like 'Nothing Else Matters' also moved me. Mr Metal and I hooked up in a big way. He was my first real boyfriend, lover and muse. We both began writing about each other.

It was in his band's drummer's backyard that I had my first recording experience, but I dread to think what that would sound like now as I don't think we had much kit. I think maybe we only had a cassette recorder. Nonetheless, it was in these passionate teenage years that realised I was committing to the path of a singer and I would do whatever it took. Yes, I was seduced by the images the media sold us: the big mega-star success, the limousines, the mansions, masses of screaming fans, arena tours, all that attention. I was drawn by the flash, snap, snap of the paparazzi's cameras. It looked thrilling and exciting and I wanted it. I was also getting hooked on America's latest recording sensation, NWA. This 1980's hip hop act was breaking laws and chart records. Their hit track 'Fuck the Police' landed right on the money in my book. I was relieved that through music and the rebellion of mass rebel fans worldwide, I too was finding my voice. These guys were mega successful and they were not obedient, so maybe I didn't have to be either.

In fact, I was starting to think that maybe the religion I had been sold was not – pardon the pun – the Gospel truth. The more I was surrounded by eccentric teachers, artists, and musicians, the more I realised there was a plethora of life choices and sexual orientations. Maybe, just maybe, this whole Christian Brethren thing was not actually what it was cracked up to be. I was starting to see things differently.

I began going to church less and less, but there was still a foreboding sense of panic every time Mr Metal and I made love. I would often wake the next day choked with fear, every fibre in my body in shock, convinced I would be punished immeasurably for extramarital sex. I feared a punishment in which women could be outcast and excommunicated from the Brethren Church. These morning panic attacks existed for over a year, and of course I could never tell my parents what was going on. They were worried. They felt I was turning my back on the Lord and I know there were constant prayer meetings among their friends that I would repent and return from the error of my ways.

"Train a person in the path in which they should take, and when they grow they will not turn from it." This was a Bible verse that my father would quote at me at every meal. I was still living under their roof, and dinnertime began with a prayer. There were regular Bible readings, but I was becoming noticeably absent and listless during these forced sessions. My double act was waning, and I couldn't be bothered to keep up my girl-next-door façade.

One day, completely unexpectedly, I received the biggest blow of rejection I had ever been dealt.

In the post came a letter addressed to me.

It looked ominous, and as I opened it my hands trembled.

I read it once and then had to read it twice.

The letters stood out, stark, accusing. Each one tore a strip from me.

"Due to fornication in your life", it read, "we are no longer permitted to associate you."

My heart sank and my stomach collapsed. Inside, the part of me that had shut down was dealt another sharp blow.

The words left me breathless. These people who had reared me since I was a child were cutting me off. I was excommunicated.

And funnily enough, it hurt like hell.

I was devastated at getting excommunicated and I felt totally bereft, but at the same time I was glad I wasn't going to have to live a charade any more. My parents were stunned. I think it hurt them that the group could be so harsh, but we never discussed it. I was too ashamed and felt that I had brought shame on the whole family.

I finally graduated from high school and made it to university. What an accomplishment. It was a difficult transition because Mr Metal and I parted ways. Our lives just took different paths. I chose a university near home as I wasn't ready to move out, leave the fold, and tackle a degree all at the same time.

It was in the latter years of university that it happened.

I met someone new.

We met through my cousin.

We met in a nightclub.

He was a DJ and I'll call him DJ Digital. We met in, well, extenuating circumstances. But would you expect anything less from me? This was my first foray into clubland and, in fact, my first experiment with Ecstasy. I don't know how my friend and I purchased it, but suddenly one night she and I were in the toilets deliberating the appearance of this melted little capsule. I mean, could it do anything? Would it do anything? It looked minute and misshapen. It had been in someone's pocket for too long and the heat had partly dissolved it. I wasn't convinced we had spent our $70 that wisely to be honest, but I was feeling reckless and rebellious. So, we divided it in half and swallowed. We promised we would look out for each other and be ready to leave if it was too much for either of us.

Suddenly, I found myself on the podium. I was weightless. It was the first time I felt her, this wanton seductress. She began taking over. I swayed my hips and raised my hands above my head, caressing the inside of my arms. The music was pounding through the sound system, but the beats and the bass were reaching me in ways I had never felt before. This feeling was deeper but familiar, like the wooden vibrations in the depths of a chord progression on the piano. A new, amplified flood of sound was seeping into my bones; my heartbeat was pulsating and speeding up to match the rhythm of the four-on-the-floor house beat. The hypnotic loop of the singer's voice beckoned. I was there for hours, lost in the strobe light, flying on a different plane.

This was bigger than me. Bigger than everything. I was on fire. I wanted to be touched and I wanted to touch everyone and everything. I don't remember who or how, but I found myself enmeshed on a sofa with at least five people.

Fingers explored, hands held mine. My face and hair were stroked. I was everywhere and nowhere, everything and nothing, all in the same moment. I had never felt so alive. It was here that I found my DJ.

DJ Digital liked the seductress in me, and she liked him. He whisked me off my feet and, in the weeks afterwards, I would be introduced to his family. Soon I found the freedom I had longed for. DJ Digital came from a different way of life. His lifestyle had no rules; his household was fun and free. I loved his parents, Mr and Mrs Liberal. I owe them a huge debt of gratitude because they took me under their wing. They were the coolest parents alive. We could smoke cigarettes with them, have one (or five) beers together. We could just enjoy being normal and free. I loved everything about this new life and soon I moved in.

The drug experience, however, was not so ideal. I began displaying strange symptoms. I didn't know they were symptoms, but I knew I was not like myself. I found myself writing songs all the time, I was sleeping less, and I lost my appetite. I had to sing, sing, and sing. If I had known what I know now, I would have known that the symptoms were hypomania and I was in the first stages of bipolar breakdown.

The DJ scene was the second place I felt I didn't fit in.

The crowd were uber cool, and there was a secret code among our group. The DJ console was a revered and honoured place, not unlike the altar in a church. Only a privileged few could stand behind the decks to teach their congregation. The people on the dance floor were their subjects, the records their religion. In our DJ group there were a range of personalities, but one in particular stood out. He was DJ Shadow.

DJ Shadow was one of the best DJs I had ever heard. He had an aggressive, straight-up style of the darkest brand of tunes out there. It was even better than heavy metal. This sound hit me right in my heart and I loved every deep and menacing beat. As I had come to learn, the style of someone's instrument was indicative of their personality, and DJ Shadow was menacing by nature, too. I found him intimidating and my boyfriend DJ Digital idolised him. Many of us did, and that is why much of his behaviour went unchallenged. But I think he was, at times, a bully. I still admired him, though – I didn't have a crush on him, but I wanted to understand how he made music and I wanted to learn how these eerie female vocals were put into the tracks. It was piquing my curiosity because I knew so much about classical music and orchestration, but the electronic music scene was a minefield.

I had now left university and started a full-time job in telemarketing at one of the city's biggest media companies. Being an adult in the real world plagued my mind with fear, because I knew I had to earn money. I knew having a career and being a success was vital to keeping myself off the streets and not becoming homeless. *You must not be unemployed, Priscilla,* I told myself. *You must not.* When they announced redundancies at my day job, sleeplessness began setting in. I would wake in the night with my heart pounding, my fingers and jaw clenched. I was sure I was going to lose my job and it terrified me so much.

It was also at this time that I decided to play DJ Shadow a song I wrote for him. I went to great lengths to go to a recording studio and put down this vocal a cappella, which means the singer performs solo with no other musical instruments. I knew that DJs could use vocals over music, because they often talked about getting the a cappella B-side of a record.

It was cool recording in a studio. It was only my second recording experience, and my voice was getting stronger. I had even won a few talent quests by this stage, but while recording this second time it happened again. I was still getting that pain in my throat when I tried to hit the high notes. My voice would physically choke and get stuck. It hurt to sing. I would push through it to record, but often I had to cough and clear my throat. Something just wasn't right.

Nonetheless I was happy with this recording, and I took the a cappella of my song – for DJ Shadow, about DJ Shadow – to the one and the same DJ Shadow.

He worked in a record store, and the counter stood on a raised platform. So once again he towered over me from a height while I talked to him. I felt somewhat like Oliver, my favourite musical character in the famous *Oliver Twist* scene. I went into the shop timidly, just to play my idol this song. As I held up my CD to his face, I managed to squeak out, 'I wrote this song for you.'

I don't think I chose my timing correctly, but I also don't think he was particularly tactful. He looked at the CD inquisitively, and then to my delight and horror he put in into the CD player and began playing it out loudly over the big sound system.

He started trying to mix it into a track with just beats, and I was delighted to hear my voice over some electronic music. But then something went disastrously wrong.

He stopped. He looked at me and said flatly, 'This is out of time. I can't use it.'

He was almost violent in his reaction, throwing the CD away from him with disdain. I was shunned.

It felt like I had been slapped in the face.

I retreated.

I shrank.

And part of me broke ...

I ran home and cried the most soul-wrenching tears I have ever cried. I had a fitful night of sleep and woke to tears involuntarily streaming down my face. I was utterly shattered. My fragile inner artist had just experienced the harshest, unfettered rebuke, and all my self-belief blew up in my face. I went through the rest of the week like a ghost. I barely spoke and barely ate.

That weekend we all gathered at our favourite night spot, Club Danger. DJ Shadow was going to be playing, but I could barely meet his eye. I took a pill, hoping to escape and drown my sorrows. But something unforgettable happened. As DJ Shadow began banging out a vindictive set of unrelenting aggression, I fell to pieces. I began sobbing uncontrollably. I could not collect myself. Some people tried to console me, but it didn't work.

Later I remember DJ Shadow coming to find me in the toilets. I think he wanted to apologise, but I was too far gone, and nothing made sense. A dear friend, the eldest person in our group called Guardian Angel, took me outside. As I cried and cried I told Guardian Angel everything – how all I wanted to do was sing, how my parents had this fucked-up religion that was choking the life out of me, how I was working a stupid job I didn't want but I needed to survive. It all came blurting out. He was the biggest bear of a man, and he wrapped me up in a hug. 'The sky's the limit for you, doll,' he said. 'You'll get there.'

That night DJ Digital drove me home, but something inside me had cracked. I didn't return to normality and I stopped sleeping.

The next day the door slammed and I looked at Mrs Liberal, DJ Digital's mum. 'He's just shot himself,' I said. I was clearly in the early stages of extreme paranoia. Everything was overwhelming; it was like living in a horror movie with the soundtrack turned up on full volume. All my senses were on high alert, and I was anticipating and believing in imminent death and disaster.

Mrs Liberal looked at me with tears in her eyes. 'No, dear,' she said. 'He just slammed the garage door.'

I wouldn't believe her, so she took me downstairs to show me the garage. She then took me to my mother, crying all the way. My mother was very teary, too. She had been worried for years, as she had noticed that not only was I straying from God, but I was generally demonstrating strange, erratic behaviour. This breakdown was a build up over time, and she was distraught. It has made me realise that supporting someone with a mental illness is rough. Sometimes it can cause carers to have their own mental health crises. It is a vicious circle.

Things began to change. Everything felt like a trick, like I was trapped in a computer game. The headlights on cars at night meant that agents were spying on me. The red light would glow ominously on the microwave and TV and I knew I was being watched.

I was being recorded.

When I went to the public toilets, the male and female symbols on the door were part of an intricate game. My life and the lives of everyone I loved depended on the choice I made.

My mother took me to see a doctor, but I was convinced that this was all part of an elaborate ruse. Secretly I knew what was going on, but I was playing along with the game. To my distorted mind, they were planning something special.

Another one of our friends had moved to London; his name was DJ Real Deal and he had gone to record in the big music studios next to stars like Kylie. This is what I thought the whole surprise was really about. The doctor took one look at me and I told him I knew that this was really a surprise. I showed him my bag of nightclub clothes.

In hushed tones he called my mother in. With gentleness in his eyes, he told her quietly to take me to that special place they had talked about. I knew what he meant. This was why I'd packed my nightclub clothes. I knew that this place that looked like a hospital was part of the surprise. I knew I was going to London to meet DJ Real and sign a recording contract. There was a plane and limo waiting ...

As my mother took me in the car, my mind was whirling with the possibilities and what I thought lay ahead. When the car stopped, we both walked outside to the front of a building. This next building also looked like a hospital, but I wasn't worried. This was part of a grand scheme and I was being tested. All I needed to do was crack the code. I winked at the nurse at the front desk and said, 'I'm here now. I'm ready.' As she took me from my mother I heard her whisper the words "involuntary patient".

It wasn't until the nurses stuck a needle in my arm and put me on the scales to weigh me that I realised I wasn't going to London. There was no plane and no way out. I was being sectioned and I was losing my mind.

I let out a blood-curdling shriek, one so violent that I frothed at the sides of my mouth. The nurses were kind but immovable as they held me down.

When my outburst slowly subsided, they put me in a gown and locked me up.

Behind a huge glass window.

I was now an impatient patient in a psychiatric ward.

CHAPTER 4

BABY'S GOT A TEMPER

'Give me my medication
Take the edge off this frustration
'Cos I'm flying
And I'm trying
To come down'

Bipolar, Sapphira

I spent many hazed days in the high dependency unit of this psychiatric hospital, behind a thick window with other very unwell patients. We were all locked in there for our safety, but I did not feel safe. Patients would howl, tormented with delusions throughout the long sleepless nights. Other women in my ward had bandages around their wrists and I could only imagine the horror they had bestowed upon themselves. My sister would visit and leave crying. It hurt her to see my listless form, hair matted and uncombed, my pupils the size of pinholes because of the chemicals keeping me under sedation.

I was trying to find a shred of normality. It was difficult to focus, because the medication I was taking was so strong that it made my thought processes slower than normal. This added to my overall confusion. When I tried to read, an activity that normally relaxed me, I found that I couldn't. My vision was affected by the medicine. When trying to read the text on the page, all I saw was a blur.

Perhaps this was the Hell the Christian Brethren had warned me about, should I ever stray and displease God. I could only imagine them all gathering and gleefully gossiping about my demise. Perhaps they thought I had been possessed by demonic spirits as the punishment for my sinfulness.

The daily routine in the hospital was scary. Some patients had electric shock treatments. Others had severe reactions to their medication, their faces puffed like distorted balloons. My worst nightmare was soon to come. In denial and revolt, I refused to accept my incarceration. My hysteria mounted. I would scream and throw my limbs about in a fit. I was inconsolable and violent.

Who did they think they were, locking me up?

Could they not see I wasn't one of the insane ones?

I was not like the rest of these psychos. I was normal. There was a mistake.

I shrieked and screamed so loudly the nurses were at a loss. I was disrupting everyone and everything. It was decided that I should be locked in a room by myself until I settled.

Now, locked in a new and unfamiliar room, my hysteria grew to an even more unbearable crescendo. 'Let me out!' I screamed, banging at the door. 'LET ME OUT!'

But no one did and no one came.

The witching hour arrived as night set in. Ghoulish shadows danced on the walls; the hands of monsters were reaching out to get me. It had been terrifying being in the main ward in the dark, but now I was locked in this place by myself. Fear engulfed me like a ravenous flame, devouring every ounce of calmness within me. My heart was thumping, my mind racing wildly.

I desperately needed to use the toilet. I held on for as long as I could and once again banged on the door.

'Someone please, please come and help me!' I called out. My voice was hoarse with shouting. I waited and waited but no one came. And so, in sheer agony, I had no choice. I stripped the pillow case off the pillow and urinated in it.

I felt disgusted with myself, debased like a feral animal. I retreated, sobbing in total despair. Part of me died that night. My soul was in anguish. I had slipped into the deepest abyss, a place only the lost and abandoned will ever know. Incapable of words, I became pain and my soul cried out.

And it was here, in this darkest of hours inside this house of horrors, that I crossed the gates of Hell and danced with the devil. It was a total spiritual collapse, as if I left this realm and my spirit was lashed red raw. My essence, the very fabric upon which I was created, was banished from existence.

I woke the next day as the nurses opened the door to come and find me. They were gentle women. I saw sympathy in their eyes as they talked to each other, shaking their heads as they realised the state of my soiled bedclothes and linen. I was sent back to my ward where I had a private room.

I had been permitted a CD player and DJ Digital had brought a collection of my favourite CDs to have with me. The electronic dance music scene was at its peak, and I was in love with the combination and fusion of genres. Some of my favourite albums were *Way Out West, ECSM* by BT, *The Fat of The Land* by The Prodigy, and Leftfield's *Leftism*. I loved these albums for the way they blended modern electronic beats and synthesis with orchestration and piano.

One particular disc fell into my hands: *Café Del Mar Volume Tres* complied by Jose Padilla. This was a series of ambient chill-out compilations that had been circling our DJ group. A lilting melody came on as this disc played. The song was called 'Tones' by Nova Nova.

Through the speakers a beautiful piece of piano found me. It reached out and caressed my face, soothed my brow and nurtured every cell in my body. I felt it first in my heart and then it spread like a warm glow all over me. My veins opened, and I was hungrily absorbing each sweet nourishing note intravenously, starved for sustenance. I was so anchored to the piano, and without my own keyboard or place to vent about all that was happening to me, I was calmed to the very core by this music that had seeped into the room and into my body.

I knew if I had this, I could find my way back.

My silent prayer had been answered.

An angel, or something very like one, had found me.

Eventually my medication began to work, and I was moved to the less enforced area of the hospital.

It was a slow recovery, but I vowed I would find myself again.

DJ Digital stuck by my side throughout this whole saga. His loyalty and compassion helped me to pull through. My best friend Boo Boo also visited and tut-tutted when I told her how difficult I was finding being hospitalised. She consoled me, and was a ray of shining light in the murky quagmire of institutionalisation.

DJ Shadow also came to see me. I felt too wobbly to deal with people from the real world, but I was not able to refuse visitors, so I had to do my best to try to make conversation. I was particularly nervous about seeing DJ Shadow because I didn't know how to react. I still felt hurt about his reaction to my song. We made polite conversation, but it was hard for anyone to be relaxed when visiting me in the hospital because other patients would do strange things and make strange sounds. There was no privacy. I appreciated that he did make the effort and I think it shows he cared.

I knew I wasn't quite right yet, and I didn't want anyone seeing me like this except my family, boyfriend, and best friend. Thankfully any offers of visits from the Brethren Church were forbidden by my mother, who told them I needed quiet repose and rest. It angered me knowing that – after everything they had put me through, including excommunicating me – they were now trying to get in touch during my darkest hour. I was certain that they were whispering about my demise among themselves, saying that it was a sure-fire sign that I was cursed and had strayed like Lucifer turning his back on Heaven.

Seconds stretched into minutes, minutes into hours, hours into days. An excruciatingly long time lapse was in play and everything seemed to be going in slow motion. I yearned to be well enough to return home, to wake up and realise that this had all been a bad dream. But there was no escape. This was my reality, and I was living out my worst nightmare.

Finally, the day arrived when I was released and permitted to return home.

I was so shaky when I walked through the front door of our house. My legs felt weak and I was easily overwhelmed by the smallest sensations. I used to love having long baths, but even sitting in the heat of the water – with steam and bubbles rising up and around my head like a halo – made me feel queasy. I was so delicate and fragile. My eyesight blurred and I would become unsteady on my feet. It was as if I was experiencing everything again for the first time, with the eyes and ears of a newborn child. Life felt amplified and exaggerated. I was confused and intimidated by this new world.

I didn't know why I felt so unsteady. 'Your body has been through a big shock,' the doctor told me.

Learning daily tasks again, such as making a cup of tea, made me feel like an infant. I had support, with regular visits from the CAT (Critical Assessment Team). These visits were reassuring, and they helped me to realise that I wasn't alone. Many other people went through similar breakdowns.

They told me that mine was most likely triggered by the use of drugs, and that it was normal for this to occur in someone my age. I wish I had known of organisations like *beyondblue* at this time, who have great support groups. If I had been connected with other people going through this, I would have had a lot more comfort.

I began regular appointments with Dr Sanity, a psychiatrist. He put me on lithium to regulate my mood, help me regain focus and stay calm. But I felt like I was living life with the mute button switched on. The little white pills made me totally numb, like I was flatlining. I had no zest, no spark, none of the former pizazz that had always defined my personality. I was bereft of all sense of my former self, and I felt I lived life like a blurry shadow. There was no focus, no edges. Nothing brought me back to who I was.

If this was not hard enough, there was also the utter shame of facing people in my social group, work, and community again. I did everything I could to avoid having to associate with anyone I knew, but I could only hold off the real world for so long. Eventually I would have to see these people and look them in the eye.

My colleagues at work were amazing. They said I was welcome to take as long as I needed to recover, and I could return whenever I needed to. But I didn't want to know what the group at Club Danger were saying about me. There was a whisper the nightclub promoter did not want me to come back. I had been a focal point of that small group and a noticeable personality, so this catastrophe had set tongues wagging – and not in my defence. Rather, I got the sense I was being further ostracised. I heard rumours that the promoters thought it would be better if I stayed away.

I lost all self-confidence.

Completely. Every ounce.

I stopped writing music. I stopped playing the piano.

I stopped singing.

I was miserable. I had lost everything.

Every morning I would sleep until late, unwilling to face the day ahead. My mother would rouse me out of bed and bring my medication. I knew I needed to take it, but I never got used to it. The lithium tablets were thick and chalky. They had a peculiar taste and seemed to get stuck in my throat. It was horrendous.

When I returned to work, I would get to the office and struggle to find the zest I once had in my voice while telemarketing. People had always responded well to my sprightly personality over the phone. 'Smile while you dial,' they had always said in those training sessions, but I couldn't. I was flat, muted by the lithium, trying to understand who or what I was now that this had happened to me. I would eat my meals, but everything had lost its flavour. I hoped with each passing day I would find a way to get my spark back.

All the dreams I had wanted to fulfil as a singer / songwriter vanished. I could not see any way in which I could do that now. I had no songs to sing and no voice left to sing with. Of course, I could still speak and make sounds, but my desire to sing – the joyous light in my soul – had been snuffed out.

I moved through my life and undertook the duties expected of me, but I wasn't fooling anyone, least of all myself. I was just going through the motions.

To signify my trauma and grieving, I had to make a change. I cut my hair and I pierced my tongue. I adopted the butterfly as my symbol of transformation, thinking that if I could overcome this, I could overcome anything.

I wanted to stop feeling like a shadow of my former self. I didn't know who I was nor whose life I was meant to be living now. Without my pizazz and spring in my step, I felt robbed of life. I was flatlining, but I plodded on with a general stoicism that my upbringing had instilled in me. Our kind just kept going and did what was required. Things would get better somehow.

All the while I would listen to 'Tones', the beautiful song that had been my lifeline in the hospital. It became the soundtrack to my life. Just as before, each time I heard it, it brought me peace.

I knew I would find my way back because I had this piece of music to comfort me.

It took a year to return to normality, and slowly my friends and family began helping me integrate back into my normal life again.

After enduring such an upheaval, it was a miracle that my relationship with DJ Digital lasted for several long years after I was released from hospital. His family had given me a home full of unconditional acceptance and love. There was no judgement in this family, and I could be myself. It was a huge relief, and I often quizzed DJ Digital's mum about her life and lifestyle choices. She would let me drive her car and we would have drinks together. The family slowly introduced me to new foods such as seafood. They cooked English breakfast. I loved it in that place. It was a refuge for a few strays like me. Friends of DJ Digital's brothers also seemed to use the place as a landing pad. Some nights the whole house was filled with people staying over on the sofas, spare beds and bean bags. We would have fantastic house parties and big cook-ups in the morning. They also had really relaxed values around sex, and everyone openly discussed their sex lives. It was carefree and fun.

But sadly, eventually, DJ Digital and I realised that we were growing apart. It was hard to leave him because I had built a dependency on him after my breakdown, but eventually I knew it was time to find my inner strength and move out on my own. In many ways it was the extra support I got from his parents, Mr and Mrs Liberal, that also made it hard to leave. I had adopted them as my parents and I loved them so dearly and deeply.

As I planned how to end the relationship, I fidgeted nervously with the metallic silver wings of the butterfly ring on my finger. It was a gift from my sister that I wore for good luck. It comforted me as I planned how to divide our possessions and thought about what life would be like "out there" on my own.

I had entertained the idea of going overseas since childhood. Those crackly phone calls to my English relatives when I was growing up had always piqued my curiosity, but my love of dance music meant I was also reading avidly about the explosion of super clubs in London and across the UK. I wanted to experience the music culture in the capital city for myself.

As circumstance would have it, all things happen for a reason. I soon found myself living in a two-bedroomed unit that I rented by myself with a female flatmate. Being single was fun after a six-year relationship, and I began to think that maybe now it would be a good time to take that overseas trip I had always planned. Almost as soon as I had that thought, the opportunity created itself. I couldn't believe what lay around the corner.

CHAPTER 5

JERICHO

*'See, I have delivered Jericho into your hands, along
with its king and its fighting men.'*

Joshua 6:2

Do you know that feeling of déjà vu?

Have you found yourself pulled back to certain places, time
and time again? As if to conclude an energetic wave length, to
complete a cycle, to make an opening and then a closure? Have
you ever felt like you've come full circle?

I feel this way, and there are several locations to which I found
myself returning. Upon each visit I have fulfilled profound life
events in those same coordinates. It intrigues and fascinates
me. It's as though, in this web of time, we weave a tapestry, a
co-creation of destiny and choice, fate and fruition.

London was a destination I had heard about many times.
Most notably, it was the city that all the famous Australian
stars had moved to to get their big break. Kylie, Nick Cave
and Natalie Imbruglia had all launched their music careers
by relocating to England's capital city. I was also amazed by
Madonna. Her provocative music videos like *Justify My Love* and

the accompanying book, *Sex*, had given her an infamous profile in the Brethren Church. She often toured to London, and I knew the bigger artists had bases in this creative capital city along with New York and Las Vegas. I felt that one day, I, too, would move further ashore to pursue my dreams.

However, I had heard stories in detail about Great Britain long before I had even been acquainted with pop culture icons. I have mentioned my dear old dad was, himself, English. Don't get me wrong, my dad has now deferred to the Aussie lifestyle. He even wears an Akubra, the traditional Australian farmer's hat. He loves being Aussie, but he is also proud of Britain. He loves British comedies, and I still love listening to his infectious, deep fits of giggling when watching shows like *Yes, Prime Minister* or *Monty Python.*

'You can't beat British humour,' he says. And I agree!

He would often recall stories from his childhood to us, especially when we complained about getting out of bed in the winter. 'You think this is cold, kids?' he would ask. 'When I was a lad, it was so cold at school our milk used to freeze in the bottles. *And* we still had to get up and go to school. We never had heating on in the mornings; I would have cold showers. You kids don't know how good you've got it.'

My sister and I would look at each other behind his back and roll our eyes. I would mouth his words – 'you don't know how good you've got it' – in perfect sync with him as he spoke. It would always send my sister into fits of giggles. It was during these long lectures about England that he would take us to the huge world map stuck up in our dining room and point out this tiny speck of a country. Though small in size, its grandeur still made its mark, for this was the home of my ancestors, my heritage, my lineage.

We would also receive cards and updates from my dad's sister. My aunty lived in Portsmouth and would write to us both every birthday with amazing punctuality. She has never missed a birthday. There would always be English pound notes tucked into the cards. What a great and wondrous experience. It taught us at a very early age about the enterprise of international currency and exchange rates. (This was a schooling I was grateful for when I began managing international business in the corporate world and then later on in my own ventures.)

Our aunty and nan would send us regular letters and photos from England, too. In one such photo I was alarmed to see my young cousin sitting on pebbles in her bathing suit. 'Why does her beach have rocks, Daddy?' I asked. As Aussie kids, the beach was our second backyard and I had only ever seen the white sandy shores of the Australian coastline. How could you sunbathe on pebbles or make a sand pillow or sandcastles? It perplexed me no end.

Our darling nan braved the 24-hour flight and came to Australia to visit us several times when I was a youngster. I loved the delicious Werther's Original toffees she would bring in her handbag.

Occasionally, as it was a great expense in those days, we would all gather around the family dial phone that had a long, wriggly electric cable and have phone calls with our family from England. It was always quite difficult because there was no loudspeaker function, which is commonplace on home phones these days. We would have to crane our necks to hear the voices of our nan, aunty, uncle, and cousins. They all spoke with such beautifully strange accents that were unfamiliar to my ear, but I enjoyed the sound very much. To me, accents have always had a kinship to music; their timbre, pitch, and tone decorate conversation in a magical orchestration of spoken word. I could listen to people who speak with an accent talk for hours and never get bored. It's one of life's secret pleasures.

Thus, as I had such close family connections to the United Kingdom – and since I was also the recipient of dual citizenship in both Commonwealth countries – it seemed inevitable that I would one day relocate to the Northern Hemisphere. As I made plans to travel to London, my motivations were now two-fold. I not only wanted to develop a relationship with my kin and family, but I also had an undeniable twinkle of stars in my eyes. The fog of my depression was slowly lifting, and it felt like Melbourne had nothing left to offer me. Every street corner was familiar, and no aspect of the nightlife culture excited me any more. I had been there and done that. It was time for a change.

I had watched in wonder as Kylie Minogue, the girl-next-door TV personality from *Neighbours,* had been catapulted to stardom after arriving in Europe. I was certain that if I made the same brave move, the industry would surely take notice. Perhaps I should have set my sights slightly higher than shoop-shooping with crimped hair to the 'Locomotion', but if anyone could Locomotion, I could do it with the best of them! I had that sheer determination.

So, armed with my first demo of my songs on CD, I packed my life into a suitcase and threw myself headlong into this daunting adventure of moving overseas. Thanks to my day job in sales, I had learnt about territory management and new business, so I approached this manoeuvre in the same way. I asked the CEO at work to make contact with the same branch in London and send them a reference on my behalf. I made a list of everyone I knew in London, putting everyone's first name, surname, email address, postal address and phone number into a spreadsheet. It helped that DJ Real Deal was living in London, and while we were not close personally, I knew his sister well; she was living in Westbourne Grove. She was one of the first people I advised of my impending arrival and it just so happened she also knew of my aspirations as a singer. She kindly said she would introduce me to some people when I got to London.

In the Bible there was the story of Joshua. He took up arms to conquer Jericho, one of the almighty cities, and won. I was like Joshua, London was my Jericho and I was determined to conquer it. I would not let it conquer me.

As I cleared out my cupboards to reduce my belongings, something else began to happen. It was as if every discarded item represented my old life. It was heavy baggage that I no longer needed. I was stripping my wardrobe back and stripping myself back at the same time, down to the bare essentials, down to the foundation layer. And I as threw out these excess things, I threw caution to the wind. Transformation. Getting on that plane and stepping into the unknown meant that I would be taking up a new mantle. I was going to go for this, no matter what the cost. I was going to rebuild a new me in London, and I was going to be a singer. Nothing would stand in my way. I felt like a pupa in the chrysalis, preparing to emerge from my cocoon.

I had booked my ticket to London well in advance and paid for it. Having that financial commitment bolstered me in moments of major self-doubt. It's natural for most people to feel uncertain when facing a major relocation to a new country, but I was battling with more than the usual jitters because I was terrified I would relapse and have another bipolar episode if I put myself under duress. I worried about healthcare. If I had a relapse in London, who would look after me? What would the mental health care system be like? Would there be austere insane asylums like the ones I had seen in the movies? Would I have help or be locked up permanently? What if I ran out of money and couldn't get home? All these thoughts plagued me.

I had several check-ups with Dr Sanity as I planned the move. I had been off medication for over a year, but I wanted to be sure he thought I was of sound enough mind to cope with such an upheaval. He gave me the green light, but advised me to always be my own best judge of character and to listen to myself no matter what.

Butterflies had become my mascot since my breakdown. I surrounded myself with them in my home, and whenever I saw one in my natural environment, it was a sign. I would be looked after.

And so it began. I said my farewells and before I knew it I was on a plane up, up, and away off to the UK.

On the flight over I was wretchedly sick. I felt sorry for whomever was sitting next to me. The finality of leaving my home country for what felt like forever seemed to take a physical toll on my body. It was if the expulsion of everything I had ever eaten was part of a cleansing of my heart and soul. After vomiting severely and making several trips to the toilet, I finally managed to sleep.

I arrived into London on an unseasonably balmy summer's day and was immediately comforted when I caught the bus past Burgess Park in Camberwell. The grand entrance to the park was an archway that stretched up and over the path. It had the most extraordinary and intricate mural of a butterfly pattern. I breathed a sigh of relief, a long exhalation. I was going to be alright. I had been led here.

As I arrived into London, the ancient buildings and bustling energy excited me. I loved the architecture, the colours, the intermittent splashes of red as I passed a double decker bus or post box on the corner of the street. There was something charming about London; history echoed out from the walls of every building. I felt a strange sense of homecoming. It was wonderful and energising. I felt free.

It was so warm on this blustery day. I marvelled that the temperature was a record 30 degrees Celsius. I had only ever envisaged the city to be a wintery, grey mass.

DJ Real Deal's sister was true to her word and promised we would go out so that she could introduce me to some people. It felt nice having some familiar faces from my hometown in this huge new metropolis. It meant that I had some people to turn to should anything go awry. They knew my culture and my background and could look after me if I needed help.

'There's someone you should meet,' DJ Real Deal's sister said. 'He's very connected in the music business and he manages several famous bands & DJs.' My interest was piqued. Could this be it? Could my big break be happening so soon? I could barely believe my luck.

I had carefully created 10 demo CDs back home. They were very rough, and I had used instrumental tracks from CDs I had in my car to write my own songs over the top. I'd managed to persuade a graphic designer to donate his skills and was quite pleased with the CD cover we had created, too. I took all 10 discs in my bag that first night out in London – I wanted to be prepared. I think my business and marketing training has served me well; I always have some kind of collateral at the ready in my handbag to share should the right industry executive pop into view. I didn't just leave it at the demo CDs; I decided on the perfect see-through blouse and smart pants combination that showed the outline of my bra. It was inviting without screaming "come-fuck-me" too loudly.

So, we set the scene of my first visit. It was a part of London that has since become a revolving door of life-changing events and meetings. The location is North London. The place is The Spot.

DJ Real Deal's sister was the lady about town. With a brother whose name meant she could get on any guest list at the hottest nightspots, she was the perfect chaperone for my first night in London's world-famous nightlife scene. Even on the distant shores of Melbourne, reports of the notorious rave scene – with lasers and heaving masses of people on the dancefloors – had made primetime news in Australia. I had read several books on nightlife culture and knew that London was the heartbeat of a cultural revolution. And so it was that we found ourselves at The Cross. Set in a derelict industrial estate, the warehouses had been converted into high-end nightclubs with booming sound systems split across several rooms. There was an electric atmosphere as we waded our way through bodies that were heaving and grinding in time to the heavy hypnotic house beats.

DJ Real Deal's sister forged on ahead, turning back to make sure she didn't lose sight of me. At last we arrived in the furthest room of the club. As the crowd thinned out a bit we had space to breathe and could finally hear each other.

'Oh, I can see him! Come on,' she said, tugging my arm. 'You've got to meet him. He works with my brother.'

Lo and behold, a figure stepped out of the shadows. Our eyes met just as the music stopped and my heart stopped, too. I felt an electric jolt as his gaze locked with mine. He was not only the most prolific music industry contact I had ever laid my eyes upon, but he was also jaw-droppingly gorgeous and charismatic, with a wry irreverent smile. My knees went weak. I had found him. This was my Mr Big.

From that moment I was swept up into a whirlwind romance and Mr Big and I were head over heels in love. He was 38 and I was 25 and my world revolved around him. He was the earth and I was the sun and moon. Initially he thought it wouldn't be a good idea if I moved in with him, but after a few short weekends he and I were inseparable.

I got my first field rep job on a London sales team. It came with an amazing new hire-purchase car as part of the package. I squealed with sheer delight when the car was dropped off at the door of our home. I grabbed Mr Big by the hands with a child-like urgency. 'Quick,' I commanded him. 'Get in the car. I want to drive! Let's go to somewhere famous, a big landmark. I want to drive past something monumental.'

The two of us cruised through the streets of South London. I was glad that the English drove on the same side of the road as Australia, but I also noticed the communication between drivers on such busy road. There was lots of eye contact and cooperation, with people stopping to flash me in at a busy intersection or slowing down to allow me to cross into their lane. It was a lovely sense of camaraderie that Australian roads don't have. I realised that to get around the bustling London thoroughfares, this kind of inter-transport communication is essential. Otherwise, no one would get anywhere!

Suddenly they loomed up ahead: Big Ben and the Houses of Parliament. We crossed the Thames and went around the roundabout. I squealed again with delight. 'Eek, look at me!' I shouted out the window. 'Look at me everyone, a little ol' Australian. I'm driving in London! Can you believe it? LOOK AT ME!'

My heart swelled with pride to have landed in London and landed myself an amazing job with a company car. This beauty was metallic silver with that new car smell; it was so divine. I was on cloud nine. I had my demo CD, I had Mr Big of the music industry sitting on the passenger seat right beside me, and I was ready for the big time.

There are so many things I love about living in London, but probably the best thing of all is the proximity to Europe and the ease of popping on a flight and being in a different country two hours later – in whichever direction you choose to depart from.

After travelling 29 hours long-haul one way from Australia, this kind of convenience is a luxury. I was itching to embark on my first trip with Mr Big. He was managing the biggest Italian music band of the hour, with a hit song so famous it had even made Number 1 in Australia as well as around the world. I couldn't wait to meet these virtuosos, and best of all they had all said I was invited to record with them! They couldn't wait to hear my songs. I nearly had heart failure several times when Mr Big told me this news. Did I really have what it took to conquer the Jericho of the music industry and record with the big shots?

We arrived into Naples airport in the evening and the band were waiting for us at the gates.

'Ciao, bella,' the band leader crooned. 'Come stai? How are you?'

I smiled shyly and said hello. I felt like a fish out of water with such famous chart-topping musicians. A faint fear fluttered in the recesses of my mind. I remembered how formidable the DJ scene had been in Melbourne, and I don't think any one of those artists had even had a sniff at the Top 40, let alone a global Number 1 hit. How much more austere would this group of world-famous musicians be?

My worries were soon put at ease by the warmth and sheer care this group and their families showed me. I experienced nothing but gentle thoughtfulness of the most supreme nature, the kind of hospitality Italians are famous for the world over. 'Eat,' they would urge me at every meal. 'Eat some more.' If parmesan cheese could be administered intravenously, I am sure Italians would be lining up around the block. They smothered it on everything!

And the espresso! I had never tasted coffee so good. At the airport there were even little kits for the ardent Neapolitan coffee lovers who had to travel. The kit included locally ground coffee and a little bottle of Neapolitan water; the combination of these ingredients was so important that people could not bear coffee without their own water. I thought it was priceless. It also showed me that cultural identity with food is a real source of pride and reverence. Having come from a young country like Australia, I had not experienced this before. Australia has no historical food of its own apart from damper, the typical bushman's tucker, or the Aboriginal bush foods. I was not exposed to much of those cuisines as a child. In my family we borrowed a lot of meals from England and Germany, but Australia's cuisine is vastly multi-cultural. Italy has a pride linked to their food – they're almost as proud of their food as they are of their flag.

The band was working on a new album, so we were treated to a few of their latest tracks as we cruised from the airport to the city of Naples via Posillipo. Soon they would say "via Priscillipo" to tease me.

'What do you want to do, Preescheela?' they asked me. 'What do you want to be in the music business?'

'I want to be a songwriter,' I would say. 'And a performer. That is the only thing I want, more than anything in the world.'

'Ah, this is not the only thing in the world,' they would caution me. 'This industry, it's shit, don't let it rule you.'

I was intrigued that they would say this, but nonetheless I couldn't quell the fire burning in my heart.

Spending time in Naples enabled me to learn the essentials of the Italian language, but many of the words were familiar to me from my musical training. Italy is the language of music. All the musical charts and sheet music contain Italian instructions like *allegro* – lively – and *andante* – walking pace. Even the word "piano" itself is Italian, the true pronunciation being *pianoforte* – soft loud.

Touring Italy with the band was the best fun I ever had. I only had one tiny regret. Initially we had planned to only stay for the weekend with them but were persuaded to join the whole tour. I learnt a lesson. Italians are *très chic*. Their day-to-day style was remarkable; people would wear tailored jackets for grocery shopping and stilettos to top up the parking metre. These *ragazzi* did not slum it. So here was my dilemma. I had packed three outfits for a weekend break only, and as we were whisked away on a two-week trip, I had to recycle the same dull outfits over and over. There wasn't time to shop in the hectic tour schedule. I almost died with embarrassment when I saw sophisticated, dolled-up music TV hosts extending microphones in manicured hands while I was standing there behind the scenes, feeling unsightly. Could I not be Mr Big's flashy Australian girlfriend with a demure flick of smooth, blonde locks and designer threads instead? It was hard to hold my head high.

Still, hanging out backstage with A&R from Sony and all the media celebs was incredibly cool. I learnt a lot watching the band sound check, rehearse and prep on a busy tour schedule. I also loved the celebration of summer, a big feature at the outdoor clubs. Italy's finest glittered at pool parties. There was style, there were skimpy swimming costumes, and there were the oh-so-debonair airs and graces of the A-list, who would decorate the edge of the pool with their perfectly pristine make-up and designer detail.

You could easily identify the girls who knew you knew they were Miss-It-And-A-Bit. Miss Pretenziosa walked the distance from the bar to the pool like it was a catwalk and she was the star model on the runway. I didn't know how she managed to pose and pout to such perfection, but she did. You could imagine everyone's amusement when Miss Pretenziosa decided that parading with the casual flick of her hips around the pool's edge was not getting her enough attention. She wanted to go one better.

I have found the music industry can attract attention seekers, and can you imagine me chastising anyone for seeking such attention?

I was not feeling styled enough, in my three-day-old denim shorts, to join the promenade of model walkers. I was keeping a low profile and enjoying some people watching. This was when Miss Pretenziosa chose her moment. She circled the entire edge of the pool area in a hot pink one-piece that only just covered the essentials. She wanted all eyes on her and she had them. As one who has mastered this same skill, I was wise to her game. But I thought I should take mental notes and see if she had any tips I could borrow for a later date. Watch and learn.

In the centre of the pool there were large inflatable armchairs. They floated invitingly, and many of the models had been sunning themselves on them. Their stretched back their slim physiques, exposing toned midriffs as they perfected their tans. Miss Pretenziosa stopped with a dramatic pause and flick of her hair before reaching out a tentative foot to catch the closest armchair. It was made of hot pink plastic, just the colour of her breast-hugging one-piece. We were all watching now.

She smiled effortlessly, as if she was unaware she had the undivided gaze of everyone around the pool. But she was. Casually holding her mobile phone to her ear, she continued in a private conversation. This allowed her ample time to laugh privately and smugly. Every man in the room probably wished it was he who had her number, that it was he who was the cause of her biting her lip as she laughed seductively.

She lowered herself into the floating armchair with the dexterity of someone who bashed out 20 reps of squats and 10 sessions of Pilates a week. She, too, arched her back to give us all full view of the perfectly toned torso and curve of her buttocks. Still engaged in conversation, she gave a deft push of her foot against the pool's edge and tilted her head back.

And then it happened.

Something went wrong, and her balance was way off.

With a curdling squeal she lost control – and the armchair flipped her face first into the water. Her Gucci glasses slid over one eye, her phone plummeted into the water and soon she was submerged. You did not need to speak Italian to understand the riotous laughter that erupted from the onlookers, including me. We hooted and cheered, whistled and hollered. This was the funniest thing I had ever seen. Miss Pretenziosa finally surfaced, mascara streaked down her face, her hair flat and wet and straggled over her body. She clutched her phone in her hand, sodden and dripping with water. She doggy-paddled towards the steps and didn't meet anyone's eyes as she clambered out of the water like a drowned rat, cursing under her breath.

And what do you know? I did learn something that day. I learnt that pride comes before a fall. (And, of course, to always match my swimsuit with my inflatable armchair.)

We were in a different city each day, a different hotel each night. That was the drill of the touring band and crew. It was a lot of stop-starting and a lot of work, but I was waiting for the moment to share my music.

One morning, as we all gathered in the reception of a hotel after breakfast, I spied a piano. I was terrified, but I thought to myself, *feel the fear and do it anyway.*

Without asking, I plonked myself at the keys and began a performance of my favourite piano composition. I could see the band's ears perk up as all eyes turned in my direction. *Breathe,* I reminded myself. As I reached the final note, I couldn't believe I had played the whole piece without any mistakes. The whole restaurant burst into applause, but the loudest claps came from the band. *'Brava, Priscilla. Brava!'* they cheered, whooped, and hollered.

I went bright pink, but I knew I had done my composition justice and I glowed with a quiet pride. 'Hey, Preeshey, you write good stuff,' said the main band producer and bass player. 'We've got to get her into the studio, no?' He gestured to the other band members. Mr Big was also glowing with pride.

My transformation into a butterfly – *farfalle* in Italian – was looming. When the tour finished we went straight to the recording studio. I would sit on the sofa in quiet awe, looking at long desks of knobs and speakers. I could not fathom what half of this strange equipment did in the musical process. The realisation that I never wanted to be a music producer began to dawn on me. Each day we would return to the studio and watch the band recording, tweaking, and fine-tuning each and every sound.

I am remiss to admit that I found it all a bit boring. We hadn't seen a single limousine or red carpet in this whole time. Maybe the music industry was also exaggerated in order to sell a dream to wishful industry hopefuls like me. The behind-the-scenes of music making was monotonous and repetitive. The studio overlooked the bay of Vesuvius, and there was a beach right outside the door. How could we spend all day in a basement with no natural light, when there was sunbathing to do? My attention soon wandered, and I eventually found excuses most mornings to escape to the beach and sit in the sun.

The guys could look down and see me from the upstairs. One afternoon, Mr Big gestured urgently to me to come up. 'The guys are stuck on a melody and I told them how good you are on piano. Can you come up and help?'

I couldn't believe I was getting invited to jam with the Italians! I eagerly dusted the sand off my feet and threw my summer dress over my bikini. As I walked up the steps to the studio, a familiar narrative began in my head. *Okay, Priscilla. This is it, you realise. You have to write a hit song in this next hour. If you get this right, you will be on the home stretch. You moved overseas for this, so you have to do it and you have to get it right. Don't fuck it up.*

The pressure of my internal dialogue was making my hands clammy and my throat seize up with anxiety. Needless to say, I was a sweaty mess by the time I reached the studio, and as the team played me the loop they were working on, I was not in the best creative mindset. *Write, I was telling myself. Play something, anything. Just do it!*

Lo and behold I froze, right there, on the spot in this dark, airless studio. I could not think of a thing. I tried to casually idle my hands over the keys of a synthesiser. I had played piano all my life, and yet somehow my fingers felt like wedges of cast iron. They were clunky and ineffectual. I wasn't used to the spring of an electronic keyboard; I had always played the ivory keys of an upright piano. It just didn't feel right and my hands were freezing. I stammered and wheezed.

They all smiled encouragingly, but it didn't matter. I was completely stuck. I don't know how long I sat there – feeling awkward, breathless and incapable of producing a sound with my voice or the keys – but somehow I was eventually able to leave. I tore out of the room with as much composure as I could muster, but I was fighting back the tears as I span on my heels. I barely made it out of the door before I broke down, my whole body wracked with deep, hacking sobs.

How could this go so wrong?

How could I ever be a singer, let alone a songwriter, if this happened all the time?

I was angry and ashamed with myself.

Another little piece of my heart broke and shut down. I felt the same anguish I'd felt when DJ Shadow hadn't liked my song. My whole world was crumbling down upon me and I couldn't let Mr Big see my tears or know my sorrow. I had to keep a bright exterior and hide behind my mask. I was expected to show my face at dinner, so I hid from Mr Big so I could dry my tears.

Later that night at dinner, the pasta and espresso were flavourless. My mouth felt like cardboard and my efforts at pretending I was carefree were laborious. I don't think I fooled anyone. I couldn't wait to get back to London and forget the whole thing. This was the worst feeling I had ever had other than the agony of my breakdown. I couldn't understand why my voice had got stuck in front of my friends when I could sing so freely in the shower. I couldn't understand why my creativity had dried up like a drought-stricken desert. This was too painful. My disappointment in myself was impossible to bear. I was my own worst enemy. A deep self-loathing set in. I didn't know how to drown it out.

CHAPTER 6

BORN AGAIN

*'Let your light shine before men, that they may see
your fine works and give glory.'*

Matthew 5:16

I had always loved dancing. And all through my teenage years I couldn't stop myself from wriggling involuntarily whenever a catchy tune came on to the radio. I didn't need an invitation. My hips would shake, and my feet would tap at the hint of a groove or the snap of a beat. Just as music came innately to me as a pianist, dancing came as naturally to my body as a musical translation.

On my 23rd birthday, before I moved to London, I fell in love with a new style of dance. Boo Boo, my best friend, knew all the best places around Melbourne for entertainment and she insisted we should have my birthday at the latest Turkish restaurant. 'The prices are amazing,' she said. 'But you will love the belly dancer. Let's do it. Just trust me.'

And so it was, as we sat cross-legged around low tables with exotic flavours of hummus, meats, and falafel tantalising our taste buds, that I felt transported to a mystical Middle Eastern scene. The fragrance of the shisha and the elegant decorated rugs and drapes that hung from the ceiling made me feel like the princess in a harem.

Suddenly the music burst through the speakers with a punctuating staccato. *Dum tek tek, dum tek.* The sound of the tabla drum was the most audible of the instruments. I tuned into the unfamiliar Middle Eastern scale as strings and cymbals joined in the cacophony. As if appearing from a mirage, there she was: the most glorious, exotic creature I had ever seen. With coins on her bra and wrists and a belt jangling around her hips she writhed and contorted in perfect syncopation with the music. It was sublime. It was everything I had wanted to understand, but I had never known how to ask. She was the Goddess of all goddesses. The Universal Goddess energy streamed from her hips, her hair, her fingertips. I was utterly entranced.

The movement was sensual, inviting, and beckoning. It was expressing something I wanted to express, a sophistication, a subtlety, a spark. This woman was unapologetic in her femininity, in the command she had over her body. I was captivated. I had to have more.

The second we left I began searching for belly dancing classes and reading all I could about the history of the dance, like an animal starved for nourishment. I became obsessed with mastering this movement. I managed to complete one term of belly dancing before my trip to London, and I feel it saved me from the depression I had experienced. It felt good to be among other women who were learning this sacred, ancient dance. Something about it was deeply healing.

Now, having relocated to London, I was even more determined that this would be my new hobby. I would perfect the dance until I could also earn money as an entertainer. In London I was exposed to such a rich opportunity to learn from the best dancers in the world. It was a cultural epicentre, and all the world's best instructors flew in or were based in the city. I began tuition with Egyptian, Turkish, and Syrian teachers. I loved the new-found freedom and reckless abandon I was discovering with movement. Like with learning the piano, it was a matter of practice makes perfect and I would patiently drill hip drops, shimmies, hip lifts, chest circles, figure of eights and arm movements until I became at one with the movement.

Mr Big found my obsession daunting. He knew I loved it more than him. It took me away from him on evenings and weekends, and I think he was nervous about dating an artist because he had worked with some "crazy" singers. But I knew he was proud when I started getting booked for shows.

Now came the next dilemma. What name to use? I needed a stage name, something exotic. All the belly dancers had the most intriguing names – Dinah, Princess Banu, Little Egypt, Asmahan. I began writing out names for myself on a piece of paper. First, I looked at the different names for butterfly in all the different languages:

Faracha – Arabic

Papillion – French

Mariposa – Spanish

There was also a nickname I had been using for several years in chat rooms and in multi-user roleplay games online. It was Sapphira.

I printed all these names out and put a photo from a belly dancing photoshoot I had done next to each image. I knew when I found the right name the picture and letters would feel complete.

It was almost instant. Certain words jarred next to the photo. They didn't feel right.

I knew this was a big decision, so I also spent time on the internet to make sure I didn't choose a common name or a name that anyone else was already using. It took several weeks to settle on my stage name. While I was still to-ing and fro-ing in my creation of this persona, I was pleased to be invited to a boat party with Mr Big. As we had lots of creative friends, I thought it would be good to get their take on why they used their own names or invented stage names. I wanted to ask them what their reasons were behind such a decision.

The summer boat parties in London are simply amazing fun, and this series of parties we would go on regularly were no exception. There was something intimate about being away from the rat race and hubbub of the streets, with just a select set of people who were like-minded and all into the same music. The atmosphere was electric. I always loved going under the various bridges of the Thames because all the tourists and passers-by couldn't help but wave back as we waved at them drunkenly and happily. This kind of energy couldn't be manufactured. It was fun and carefree. I made everyone laugh when I called the Thames Barrier the Thames Barrier Reef, getting mixed up with the famous Great Barrier Reef off the coast of Queensland by mistake.

'No, Priscilla,' chuckled Mr Big. 'There is no tropical ecosystem living among the coral here!'

Mr Big and I were sitting at the stern of the boat and chatting to a group when a new couple joined us. After the general introductions were made, I couldn't help but notice the woman, Miss Daring. She had a sultry, deep accent and was from Romania. Her voice was the perfect complement to her beauty; a dark pair of eyes flickered underneath long eyelashes. She had olive skin and was about my height.

To make polite conversation, I asked her what she was doing in London and how long she had lived in the city. 'I'm here because I am a performer,' she explained in her deep, throaty voice. 'I've been here for two years because I wanted to get experience as an artist, and there is a lot of work in this city.'

I agreed with her and mentioned I was a belly dancer and was starting to create a website and a stage name.

'Where do you perform?' I asked. 'And what is it you do?'

She smiled coyly and brought out the mobile phone that was buried deep in her jeans pocket. As her coloured nails slid down her hips and across her groin, I couldn't help the wicked thought that flickered across my mind. I was finding myself deeply attracted to her. She produced a phone and started scanning through photos to show me. I pretended to look at the images with a casual interest, but my heart was racing because in each image she was becoming more and more naked. She had an amazing body!

'What kind of place is this?' I asked. 'I have never seen anything like it. What kind of dancer are you?'

She smiled and opened her moist, ruby-coloured lips to say one word.

The word that would change the course of my life forevermore.

I sometimes think what it would be like to be able to freeze frame these life-changing moments and place them in a photo album.

My eyes focused on the contours of her pouty mouth as she spoke. 'Burlesque.'

I had never heard of it before, but I loved the way it sounded – especially the way she said it.

'Burlesque?' I repeated, checking I got it right.

'Yes, that's it,' she said. 'Burlesque. You know, you should come to one of our shows. You'd love it. Everyone gets dressed up. It's like you have stepped back in time.'

'I want to,' I said. 'I want to come.'

We exchanged numbers and she sent me the address of one of the few clubs putting on burlesque shows.

When it was time to go to the show, I agonised over what to wear. The belly dancing attire was not the right mood. This was 1920s, the Weimar Republic, flapper girls. At last I settled on a corset and a pair of fishnets with fringed underpants. The club was in Notting Hill and it was called the Whoopee Club. As I stepped through the ornate, golden entrance, I walked underneath a huge, imposing chandelier. I was entranced. Mystical creatures emerged from every corner. Girls walked down the stairs, topless but for a wire bra circling around their breasts. The female compère greeted me at the door in a top hat and tails with a handlebar moustache drawn on with eyeliner. Her lips sparkled with glitter and her eyes were ablaze, amplified by huge eyelashes. Everyone in this place looked larger than life. Couples danced in perfect rhythm on the dance floor.

I ordered a glass of wine and sipped nervously, waiting for my friend to arrive.

This was an old theatre. Everything about the patrons and performers intermingled; it was hard to tell who was who. I didn't know where fantasy met reality, or the other way around. The large velvet curtain beckoned, housing a secret behind its dark drapes. I was eager for the show to begin.

The compère who had greeted me at the door loomed up on stage as the music rose to a crescendo. 'Ladies and gentlemen, boys and girls, *Damen und Herren*,' she called in an exaggerated German accent. 'Welcome to the Whoopee Club. Please sit back and enjoy the show.'

As the curtain rose the performers appeared and I felt it again.

I felt The Pull.

It came from a deeper, more private place inside me this time.

I knew I wanted to be part of this, but it was more than that. It was as if I hadn't found this – it had found me.

This burlesque show was a heady cocktail of pseudo-erotica. Seeing the headliner of the show perform was what clinched my destiny. I feel the decision had been made without me being asked.

Her name was Immodesty. Immodesty Blaize.

Ms Blaize was an explosion of erotica and female sex. Her ample curves were unashamedly on display. She had a glorious full figure, huge bosom, and hips that shook with all that God had gifted the female species. She wore a horse's tail and with each swish and swoosh, garments went hurtling across the stage. She was on fire. Her power infused the room and touched each and every one of us.

For me it was a personal, private awakening. Even more provocative than belly dance, this burlesque artform was risqué, suggestive, and taboo. I loved it. This high stage gave the burlesque artist an elitism that the common floor of the restaurant did not give the belly dancer. Much of my belly dancing experience had been on the same level with my patrons, even when I wanted them to revere me. Immodesty Blaize commanded this respect and reverence with every snap of her gloves and flutter of her eyelashes as she peered down dominantly from her perch above.

There was something naughty and thrilling about the striptease element of this show that belly dancing did not fulfil in me. I left on a giddy high.

In the coming weeks I would join internet websites and go to as many shows as I could to discover more about this artform. I was again thirsty for knowledge. Something that had been shut down in me that felt that it was coming alive again.

I had decided on my stage name.

Sapphira.

It looked right next to my images.

More importantly, it *felt* right.

I loved the fact that the name was similar to that of the sapphire, a precious gem. I wanted to create my image around the signature royal blue in my costumes. I didn't have much for a costume budget, but I had my eye on a corset in Southampton that was aptly called The Kylie, as the one and the same famous Australian singer was touring her Showgirl show.

Costuming became my new obsession and a constant reinvention. It was an investment, too.

I was thrilled when a casting call went out online. It was an unpaid gig, but it was going to be filmed at a restaurant-cum-bar near my house in Clapham North called Lost Society. I eagerly replied to the email. I couldn't wait to debut my new act in my Kylie Showgirl costume. Mr Big was a true champion; only hours before the gig he was wiring my ostrich feathers to the staves of my DIY feather fan kit.

There is another mantra that is especially relevant to my career in burlesque: "Fake it till you make it". In this instance, I *was* going to have to fake it. I had only just finished assembling my feather fans and had never actually practised at all when I dashed out of the house to perform my first debut. I had bought nipple tassels and double-sided tape and I was particularly nervous about performing the striptease and tassel twirling.

Backstage was alive with hustle and bustle. I was thrilled to be part of this exciting underworld. Performers gossiped, others chivvied for a position in the mirror to apply the final daubs of glitter and glue, and others still had headphones in, quietly drilling their act over and over before the curtain call. There was no curtain as such in this little bar, but it had a lovely wooden floor and low beams across the ceiling, giving the venue a kind of cosy intimacy.

The time whizzed past and suddenly it was my turn to go on.

I took a deep breath and held up my fans to shield my entrance and create anticipation. The music rolled and I came alive. First one glove came off, then the other. I turned my back and writhed seductively, removing my corset. I unfastened each hook, and then I was ready for the final reveal. It was perfect. As I stood there bouncing, my nipple tassels were twirling energetically as if living a happy life of their own. The entire performance went off without a hitch!

The audience burst into thunderous applause and I felt a rush from head to foot. Something touched me deeply, gripping my heart. The baby lioness who had been shunned for wiggling her dancing tail, the wounded child who had been excommunicated with harsh rebuke, the conflicted teenager and distressed young adult, the woman whose wails in the psychiatric hospital had gone unheard, all came up inside me, one by one, to take their bow and have their moment. This wasn't just for me in my present adult form, this was for all of the representations of womanhood – at all ages – within me. I felt a profound gratitude towards these beautiful applauding people with glorious, smiling faces. I would never see many of them again, but with each clap a little piece of me was put back into place. I was being rebuilt.

It was a transformation. A new foundation. I felt whole.

Sapphira was born and I was born again.

There was no shame here. There was no retribution and no chastisement.

There was happiness and liberation. I felt totally confident and experienced a real rush of adrenaline. I was piecing myself back together.

It was a joyous celebration.

I left the stage and walked on clouds.

Once backstage, I gave a little butterfly to all the performers and promoters who booked my act. It was a thank-you to them for being part of my life-changing transformation.

I made a vow that night. I vowed I would share what I had experienced, the gift I had been given, with the world. I wasn't sure how that would transpire, but in my heart I made the commitment. I was ready to tread whatever path presented itself.

Now, rushing home from my gig, I couldn't wait to tell Mr Big all about it. When I entered our cosy flat, he was out at the football and so I flopped on the sofa. I couldn't help but notice a box of his CDs lying nearby, so I began idly flipping through them. Suddenly a disc I had not seen in years appeared in the set. It was *Café Del Mar, Volumen Tres*, mixed by Jose Padilla – the album I had adored in Melbourne all those years earlier. Entranced, I flipped the disc open and began reading the credits. There was the track list and my favourite song, 'Tones'. I hadn't heard this music since I left Australia. What was it doing in this box of CDs?

I continued reading the track list and stopped dead in my tracks. One of the other artists on the album was one of our Italian friends! I continued to read the credits, and Mr Big's name appeared in the thank-you list. Whoever would have known that this man, who was now so significant in my life, had also played a part in the creation of an album that had been my lifeline? I took a moment to let it sink in.

I couldn't believe it.

Full circle.

Finding that disc at that very moment was not an accident. I was healing, and that song that had been my lifeline was coming back to find me again.

Transformation.

I also had a break with my songwriting at long last. Mr Big was managing two DJ / producers – Audiofly. Audiofly needed some vocals and Mr Big had sent them some of my a cappellas. They loved one track called 'Circles', so we met and quickly signed a contract to release it. Little did I know they were on the cusp of a major breakthrough. They invited me to hear the song performed in London when they returned from tour to DJ. 'You have to hear our tune out, Priscilla,' they said. 'It rocks the dance floor. We just heard it played in Ibiza by DJ Sasha.'

With all the DJ friends we had, and also the Italian band, I had been hearing more and more about this paradise of electronic music known as Ibiza. It was an island about two and a half hours from London, and it was famous for its hedonistic club scene. I couldn't believe my tune was being played abroad by the world's biggest DJs. This was incredible.

The big night rolled around and Audiofly were DJing in London. They invited me and Mr Big, so we found ourselves at The Cross, the club where we had met for the first time. We were back in North London at The Spot.

Full circle.

As their DJ set rolled on, I enjoyed the selection of grooves they were playing. But none of the music sounded familiar. I was getting restless and a little bit tired.

When a new powerful booming rhythm burst over the PA system, I found myself gravitating towards the bass bins (the larger bass speakers in a nightclub system). The groove was energetic and infectious. Now I was dancing. I was so lost in the moment that when a female voice oozed over the system, I zoned out. Suddenly, I realised this powerful female voice – this dominant demanding tone – was not someone else. It was, in fact, me. This was 'Circles'. It sounded so different that I hadn't even recognised the music.

I stopped dancing in disbelief, but that didn't last long. Audiofly were pointing at me. The other dancers grabbed my hands and pulled me into the middle, forming a circle around me. Everyone started pointing at me in deep reverence and acknowledgement. 'You,' they all cheered. 'It's you!'

Again, something slotted back into place that had been stripped from me. All the hurt and rejection at the hands of DJ Shadow and the writer's block in the Italian studio was being put right. I had done it. This was my voice and, if I do say so myself, it was deadly. The track was what the DJ crowd called an absolute weapon.

It took time for the moment to register. I was so overwhelmed by the power of the song and the tone of my voice on this huge sound system. But above all, I was overwhelmed by the respect and acknowledgement of my peers on the dance floor. I took this all in, deep, deep inside me into a place within my heart.

This was bigger than me.

Bigger than everything.

I was now a published singer / songwriter, and my own material had made it into London's cool cut charts. I couldn't believe it when I picked up the printed magazine and saw the title of my track listed next to a remix by the one and only Madonna. This pop icon had been my idol, and to have my name listed in print a few lines away from hers was huge! I was beaming with pride when I took this to work to show my colleagues and friends.

Mr Big took me into Soho where a select vinyl pressing of the track was being sold. We walked straight into this uber cool West End store. This was way more chic than the provincial store in Melbourne where I had had my first catastrophic song debut with DJ Shadow. As we looked up at the walls stacked high with records, we noticed my name! I bought the 12 inch and the compilation CD. My name was even printed on the receipt as the artist. I did a little squeal and Mr Big looked embarrassed. But this was my moment, not his! I even made him take a photo of me out the front holding my record proudly.

I couldn't believe it when the record label asked me if I would like to join their DJs and sing my track live at the world-famous club Ministry of Sound. Would I ever?!

In London my best friend was a fellow Australian, Miss Media. She was the most beautiful and loyal friend. She had moved over from Melbourne at the same time as me and we had some mutual friends in common. She was commissioned as my hair and make-up artist for the show at Ministry of Sound and I bought a teensy dress for the occasion. When the big night rolled around I was nervous but proud. I was singing under my real name rather than my belly dancing and burlesque persona, Sapphira, so this felt more real and connected. I loved standing on the bar, singing my own lyrics. The crowd went wild and a man even kissed my feet in reverence. How cool! The club was packed and steamy. Everyone was dancing with their hands in the air, I was in my element.

Miss Media whooped and hollered from the back row. I knew later she would give me an honest critique, because she had an eclectic group of friends in the music industry and she frequented the members' bars around town. She also went to Ibiza every summer.

'You should come with us one time,' she would urge me. 'You'd love it.' I have to admit my curiosity was piqued, but above all I had learnt that Ibiza was, in fact, the location of Café Del Mar. The series of chill-out compilations had been growing in popularity, and because of my special connection with the song 'Tones' I had been hooked getting each of the latest albums as they came out.

Since being reacquainted with the original album I had learnt that Mr Big knew a lot of the industry over there. The Italians had regular gigs in Ibiza, too. It seemed like a tropical paradise with amazing nightclubs and DJs. What could be better?

Things weren't always great, though. The first few years settling in London hadn't been easy, and even though I had Mr Big and his friends, I still felt huge pangs of homesickness and anxiety. I would often ring my Australian friends back at home in floods of tears. I sought the familiar reassurance of my motherand father's warm voices, too. They seemed so far away, and I was very fretful. While I had improved from the horrendous depression I had had a few years earlier, I was still always governed by an overall impending sense of doom. I could not quite shake why I lived with such anxiety, but fear would regularly get the better of me. I would cry for hours to myself as a way of releasing it.

I didn't speak to others about my fear. I bottled it up and would occasionally have huge wailing fits when the anxiety bubbled up beyond my control.

Thankfully, Miss Media and I understood each other's homesickness because we had both moved over at the same time. She would come to me at the drop of a hat to keep me company, joining me at burlesque shows when I needed a friend with me. I was able to grow my network and feel less self-conscious because of her trustworthiness.

When she mentioned that her friends – who were fashion designers and stylists – were going to a club called Opium Den, I was eager to go along. It was a No Costume; No Entry fetish party and I had never been to a fetish party before.

We met in West London at the stylist's house. Everyone was getting their make-up done by a make-up artist and I was enthralled with the latex, shiny PVC and leatherware everyone was dressed in. This was a very different kind of fashion. I had my own black PVC dress, thigh high boots and leather mask, which I had decided to wear for added privacy. I didn't want to be recognisable, and the secrecy was also part of the thrill. A lot of our group had masks, dramatic backless dresses, floor-length evening gowns and gloves.

We arrived at the club in the railway arches of South London. The warehouse was industrial, made of dark blue stone. There were heavy metallic doors and grinding dark beats. I felt like I had stepped into the secret underbelly of London. A man asked if he could lick my boots and I recoiled in surprise. I was intimidated yet thrilled by the proposition.

Along with my new-found confidence came new-found sexual exploration. Part of me that had been shut off for my whole life was ready to be engaged – but was I ready for this? All those around me were wearing extravagant costumes and decadent attire. It was thrilling and unnerving. Men wore gas masks; ladies walked together tethered with dog collars. I had never seen anything like it before and I was fascinated. These outfits were not cheap mock-ups; each patron had spent considerable amounts on their looks. But it was also the style of the ensembles that was spellbinding. There was attention to detail, polished nails and diamantéd eyes. This was one of the most creative collections of costumes I had ever seen, and it wasn't just the occasional person. The entire club was attired with this level of style. We were 800 people in a decadent underworld.

I walked past an evil clown. He lowered his lashes and licked his lips, beckoning for me, but I span out of reach. I turned so suddenly I bumped straight into a magician. His velvet top hat was trimmed with ribbon and his cape was tied at the neck, exposing his naked, rippled chest and abdomen. He wore black suit pants and held a staff with a skull at the top of it.

'Hello,' I stammered. He was reposed and calm. He took his time to reply. 'Why, hello,' he said, looking me up and down steadily, as if his eyes were undressing me. 'Can I buy you a drink?'

I paused for a moment and spluttered, 'Why don't you tell me your name instead? What do you do?'

'I'm Dr Flame,' he said. 'And I'm a Master.'

'Wh-wha ... what's a Master?' I squeaked.

He explained that a Master had submissives. Would I like to meet one of his slaves?

I was in complete disbelief that anyone would ever agree to be a slave, so incredulously I agreed. Either this guy was a lunatic or he was serious, and if he was serious, I was seriously out of my depth.

Fake it till you make it, the little voice in my head urged me on. I forged on behind him, but the palms of my hands were clammy, and my heart was racing. I didn't know how to act around this charismatic Adonis with a twisted agenda. He was thrilling and terrifying all at once.

Soon enough we were in another dark corner of the club. We were joined by a curly-haired petite girl in a nurse uniform. Her cleavage threatened to burst out of the zip that held her shiny nurse outfit together.

'Meet Miss Minx,' said Dr Flame. 'Miss Minx is one of my slaves.' She smiled at me, but I think she could sense my hesitancy.

Dr Flame kept his eyes closely on my expression as he positioned Miss Minx in front of him. He reached his hands around her chest, opening the zip to reveal her pert, inviting breasts and dark nipples to me. 'Do you want to join us?' he said.

I was paralysed and aroused, scared and intrigued. But I had to leave. My fear overruled everything else. I had seen too many stories of girls on the front pages of London's papers who hadn't made it home safely. I wasn't willing to take the chance with people I didn't know, in a bizarre culture club I had only just started to explore. I didn't know what to say, where this could lead, or if I would be safe. I span on my heel for the second time that night and walked away.

CHAPTER 7

WAKE-UP CALL

*'Some discoveries change the world.
All discoveries change the discoverer.'*

K Bradford Brown

My urge to experiment with my darker side began to take hold.

Mr Big and I were sadly growing apart. My boundaries and desires were increasing as I experimented as an artist. Sapphira was taking over more of my daily life and my interlude with Dr Flame flickered daily at the corners of my mind. I knew there was an alternate world out there, and I felt trapped in a monogamous relationship. I didn't want to be censored any more. It was a heartbreaking decision, but we ended our relationship and I moved out.

He was heartbroken as I announced my departure, but I vowed to myself that the best thing we could do was salvage our friendship as and when the time was right. He soon moved on from the industry, but he has always been a dear and close friend and always will be.

I was performing burlesque frequently and was slowly building up a repertoire of acts and costumes. This was my lifeline. It was not only changing all the misconceptions I had about displaying my sensuality, but it was also demystifying sex and the naked human form. Backstage at burlesque shows was a very safe and free place, but I was initially so shy about my body and would try to nervously change under my outer layer of clothing. As you can well imagine, trying to put on nipple tassels under a bra – which is under a jumper – was impractical and difficult. I had many glitter and glue mishaps; the two materials can be disastrous if applied under clothing. If I was going to be performing regularly I needed to speed up my backstage changing routine.

I was already bringing butterflies to each show to represent and acknowledge my own transformation, though I was still in the transformation process. Slowly, at each show, I emerged from my cocoon bit by bit. I started stripping off casually, and soon it became habit and didn't bother me at all. *Why had there ever been any fuss about nude bodies*, I wondered? I felt relieved to finally be among the unashamed.

You can see anything at a burlesque show.

There are boobs of all varieties: round ones, flat ones, pert ones, huge ones.

I realised that hardly anybody's body is perfect! It was a massive relief.

I love the bejewelled merkins male and female performers used to hide pubic hair, so I had to join in.

Can you guess what my first genital decoration was?

A butterfly vagazzle!

That's right, I was bouncing around, showing everyone the diamante butterflies on my vagina. This was bliss.

This was freedom. I was coming alive again. All that angst and repression I had experienced at the Brethren Church was a farce. Bodies were fun. Private parts were to be enjoyed and could be humorous, too!

Various eccentric stage personalities mingled with the behind-the-scenes characters and crew. There were stage kitties, stage managers, sound and lighting teams, plus those capturing the imagery of such a band of exotic extroverts.

Mr Portrait was a photographer. We met backstage in a downtown bar in Soho. His muscular forearm rippled as he balanced his camera and adjusted his zoom. He spoke to me through the lens and I talked to him through the mirror, looking at his reflection as I leant forward to apply mascara and eyelashes. When he lowered the camera, I knew I wanted him. He was intelligent in his conversation and had a touch of indifference about him. I asked him if he photographed nudes and if he did, would he photograph me? When he said yes, I was already planning to seduce him.

It worked.

I began living a double life again, just like I had before when I was the perfect Sunday Christian at home and a regular girl with my friends at school. I had a full-time corporate job which I needed to subsidise my expensive hobby. My constant craving for new costumes was never sated. There were also new workshops to attend to master my technique. It all added up!

Being in the corporate world always felt a bit like an acting job. Tools like my laptop were props and my suit was a costume. I used them to engage with people to achieve a desired effect. I had to be careful and find the right corporate culture in which I could fit and truly thrive. It took some skills and self-awareness. Often, I felt like the odd one out, but I have since excelled in roles, especially in my current one.

I didn't, however, feel that I could readily share this erotic evening pastime with my work colleagues. It was exhilarating but exhausting, balancing a full-time job and taking suitcases full of costumes to the office. I would always smile politely when people at my desk job said, 'Are you going somewhere nice this evening?' I didn't dare to tell them that inside my travel case I had feather boas, nipple tassels and enough glitter to fill Wembley Stadium.

It was now 2007 and the Stop and Search policy had been implemented in London after the Tube bombings had taken place. On that day the news had reached me that London had been bombed. Thankfully I was in Barcelona, but I still remember the gut-wrenching feeling I got when I heard about it. My sister, who was also on holiday visiting from Melbourne, accompanied me to an Irish pub to watch the footage on CNN. One of the bombs had exploded at Aldgate station, which was the main Tube stop for my office. Tears smarted at the corner of my eyes when I saw wounded people being rushed from the building and emergency services putting up police lines and temporary shelters.

It was a wake-up call. A harsh jolt of reality. I had felt peaceful living in peaceful Australia. All the horrors of world news seemed to happen in far-off, distant places. Now, living in London, I realised the vulnerability of life and the evil acts mankind could mastermind. As a creative person and free spirit, I don't like the default world. I choose to avoid mainstream media and live in my own creative realm of love and sparkles, because I want to live as a positive person who is not ruled by negativity. I rarely watch the news as part of my positive mental health regime, and I surround my home with vision boards and affirmations of my dreams being realised. I feel this has played an enormous role in what I have achieved and how I have been able to recover my mental perspective.

However, on this rare occasion in Barcelona, I was compelled to watch the headlines to see what had happened in London. I was so deeply saddened. Thankfully everyone I knew was safe, but my heart broke for those who lost loved ones or whose lives were changed irreparably because of serious injuries.

How can we have such implements of horror? Imagine a world where we armed ourselves with hugs instead!

It was during a Stop and Search, as I rushed through the gates of the Tube with my trusty wheelie suitcase, that unfortunately the doors closed too soon and caught my suitcase between them. I had a new act on the go, which included a plastic cane. This was protruding suspiciously from the luggage now wedged between the two doors. *Beeeeeeeeeeeeeeeeeeeeeeeeeeeep!* A loud alarm was activated to signal that something was jammed. Heat rose to my cheeks as two male police officers walked across to inspect the commotion.

'Er, what seems to be the trouble, Ma'am?' said one of the officers. I stuttered to explain myself, but I have one of those faces that, when put on the spot, looks guilty – even when I'm not. My sheepish disposition and obviously flustered state meant that the officers asked if they could take a quick look through my suitcase. In hindsight, I think they did this more for their own amusement. I doubt they thought I actually posed any real threat. To my chagrin, they grinned in spite of themselves as I lifted a feathered corset, bejewelled underpants and nipple tassels from the bag. Ah, I was exposed! (*At least I'm not exposing myself,* I thought with a chuckle. But I soon would be ...) In a matter of minutes, I was on my way, burning crimson as I boarded the Tube a few moments later.

Now I know what you are thinking. How can an extrovert like me find displaying my costumes in public embarrassing? But it wasn't really that I was embarrassed about my costume. I just didn't like looking guilty to onlookers, plus it wasn't great having my private items on display. All in a day's work though, my sweets!

In my pursuit of self-actualisation, I fought for some opportunities hand over fist. Others landed square in my lap. The chance to teach dance classes is one such example of the latter.

As belly dancing and burlesque requires mastering props like the veil and feather fans, I had required a larger space than my own living room. It was therefore much to the delight of the body builders at my local gym that I was given permission by the gym manager to rehearse in the large group fitness room when it was not in use. Thus, I would find myself shimmying vigorously to Middle Eastern melodies and the jingle jangle of my coin hip scarf, while muscle-bound marauders deftly punched out a set of reps into the punching bag in the opposite corner of the room. It was indeed a striking contrast of activities, but in London space is a commodity. And if I had a free studio with a mirror I was going to use it, never mind the onlookers!

It was while I was wrestling, in vain, with my veil – trying to spin effortlessly yet getting more and more tangled, resulting in it hanging around my neck like a noose – that a gym trainer came in and suggested that people would love to learn belly dancing in the gym. Had I ever thought of teaching classes? I was surprised she gave me the offer, as I was nearly asphyxiating myself with two metres of Arabian silk. But I nodded my agreement and deftly untangled myself.

It was true. I was going through a deep awakening in the exploration of my performance and sensuality, and I knew I could help other women. There must have been others like me who had been shunned for displaying their feminine essence, so I leapt at the chance to teach.

I made a new commitment to turn around all the trauma of my past and use it to share my new-found joy as an entertainer. I wanted to reach as many people as possible. I had already had an epiphany, realising that I wanted to help the world using my music and songwriting. But now I knew that learning about sensuality could help others, too – especially with their mental health.

At the gym a list was put at the front desk for anyone interested in taking belly dancing classes. It quickly filled up with names, so a few short weeks later I extended my reach and shared my sparkle. I was evolving from a performer into a nurturing, caring dance teacher. This was a beautiful transition, a further transformation in my own journey. Teaching other women brought a depth of joy I hadn't experienced before in my life.

I loved the bonding in those small classes. My regulars soon became friends, and when the group really reached a moment of perfectly synchronised choreography, my heart sang with happiness. It was magic.

I started doing more and more shows as a performer, too. That weekend I was invited to perform by Miss Media at the stylist's house from the Opium Den night. I recognised a few of the faces from the fetish club, too. I was living in a new home now and I arrived at this show single and ready to mingle!

It's funny how you find love when you're not looking for it.

As I wheeled my suitcase into the house I greeted everybody I knew. I was then escorted around to the back yard.

There he was. Mr Muscles and I locked eyes instantly and, not unlike Miss Pretenziosa in Italy, this time I was parading to get everyone's attention. I had the cutest little hot pant halter-neck suit with fishnets, and my make-up was done Sapphira style. I fluttered my false eyelashes at everyone in the room, engaging anyone who tickled my fancy in a brief flirtation. My gaze kept being drawn back to Mr Muscles. He was toned and athletic and so well groomed, I thought, *He's probably gay.* But he seemed to be fluttering his eyelashes at me in a bout of flirtatious fencing. Touché!

I looked forward to owning my stage persona and being all I could be. This Goddess was learning how to command a room. I felt in control and powerful as I preened with prowess.

It goes without saying that I teased to please at that show, and when I was done Mr Muscles could not look at anything else in the room. We wound up talking to each other and he offered to drive me home. We fell into bed. After a few short months he asked me to move in with him, but I set out a few of my own stipulations first. I had decided I'd had enough of London; it had been four years and the music industry had not come knocking at my door. I'd had a modicum of success as a burlesque artist and even some front-page news stories, but I missed home.

I missed the beach and the happy-go-lucky Aussie friendliness. The pollution, weather, and overpopulation in London was getting me down. I confessed to Mr Muscles that it would not be fair to get into a relationship if he didn't see himself relocating. I was preparing to pack my bags and go home and was only going to stay if there was some possibility we could be together in England for a year or so and then move back to Melbourne. To my surprise, he agreed. He was a triathlete and also a personal trainer. I knew that he would fit right in with the Australian sun, surf, and sport culture, especially since he was so athletic. He had family in Queensland and his best friend had a business. When he called the friend and found out the business was in Melbourne and that they would be delighted to help him and sponsor his visa, I thought my luck had all come at once.

I couldn't believe this dreamboat of a man could be true. I asked myself what planet he had come from. Where had he been all my life? It's funny how you should be careful what you wish for.

Mr Muscles invited me to live with him in Surrey, and what a transformation it was to leave London. Every day I would get up early to cycle to the gym and walk through fields of countryside with meadows and horses. It was so peaceful. I loved living with Mr Muscles and I loved his home, which soon became mine.

At the same time, I found myself in the most amazing new job. I was headhunted by the director of sales for a social media-style website of the day, before Facebook made its prolific debut. This, too, was a picture sharing website for people with social interests. He had seen my profile on the internet and could see that I was a songwriter but with current media sales experience working with the leading advertising agencies. The combination of my understanding of the dance music scene as well as the media landscape appealed to him, and thus I found myself employed by the company. As I entered the building I chuckled to myself. The address was 89 ½ Worship St. I had never worked at a building with such an irregular address, but the address suited the kookiness of the company to a T.

The offices were the craziest I had ever seen. They had been designed by theatrical set designers and the upstairs was carpeted in green. There was a caravan, a prison, and a tree house. Downstairs was a nightclub and a murderer's lair with a dungeon and a meat-ing room – a play on words, because the meeting room had a huge glass-topped table through which you could see realistic moulds of meat. It was eerie and genius. Above all, right about my desk there was a huge butterfly. It felt like an omen, so I accepted the role right away. As visitors arrived at our office they were greeted by two looming gated doors and they had to press the buzzer. I had been in that same position at my first interview, nervously fidgeting while waiting for the crackling signal to alert to someone inside that I had arrived.

The doors swung open into what looked like, at first, a warehouse courtyard area. But there were interesting graffiti works on the door and a nuclear powerplant warning symbol painted on the next set of doors. At the main entrance, another buzzer had to be pressed to get into the main building. In the foyer of the warehouse office space were clothes racks. This was the dressing room, and everyone who arrived had to leave their ordinary selves at the door and put on a costume to be a different version of themselves. An exaggerated character. I loved this concept. From a Pharoah's headdress to a ballerina's tutu, there were wigs and accessories of all kinds. One person at the company even went on costume reconnaissance missions, scouring fancy dress stores and charity shops in order to add to the collection. It was constantly growing.

What I loved the most about this company was the business leader, Mr Party. Mr Party was a true creative genius who had made several successful inventions and patents, making him his fortune. Now independently wealthy, his passion was to empower people, create community, and allow people to express themselves without inhibition. I knew I fitted right in.

The biggest gift of all was still to come. After a few months of being at the company, Mr Party announced that all of us would be going on a company team-building trip to the Nevada Desert. The location was intriguing. Why would we be going to a desert? Soon he called us all to sit down and have a planning meeting. He explained that the desert was the site of one of the world's most famous festivals of self-expression: Burning Man.

My curiosity was truly sparked. We were all given a copy of the 10 Principles of Burning Man, and as I read them I felt the hairs on my arms stand on end.

10 Principles of Burning Man (Harvey, 2004)

Radical Inclusion

Anyone may be a part of Burning Man. We welcome and respect the stranger. No prerequisites exist for participation in our community.

Gifting

Burning Man is devoted to acts of gift giving. The value of a gift is unconditional. Gifting does not contemplate a return or an exchange for something of equal value.

Decommodification

In order to preserve the spirit of gifting, our community seeks to create social environments that are unmediated by commercial sponsorships, transactions, or advertising. We stand ready to protect our culture from such exploitation. We resist the substitution of consumption for participatory experience.

Radical Self-reliance

Burning Man encourages the individual to discover, exercise, and rely on his or her inner resources.

Radical Self-expression

Radical self-expression arises from the unique gifts of the individual. No one other than the individual or a collaborating group can determine its content. It is offered as a gift to others. In this spirit, the giver should respect the rights and liberties of the recipient.

103

Communal Effort

Our community values creative cooperation and collaboration. We strive to produce, promote, and protect social networks, public spaces, works of art, and methods of communication that support such interaction.

Civic Responsibility

We value civil society. Community members who organize events should assume responsibility for public welfare and endeavor to communicate civic responsibilities to participants. They must also assume responsibility for conducting events in accordance with local, state, and federal laws.

Leaving No Trace

Our community respects the environment. We are committed to leaving no physical trace of our activities wherever we gather. We clean up after ourselves and endeavor, whenever possible, to leave such places in a better state than when we found them.

Participation

Our community is committed to a radically participatory ethic. We believe that transformative change, whether in the individual or in society, can occur only through the medium of deeply personal participation. We achieve being through doing. Everyone is invited to work. Everyone is invited to play. We make the world real through actions that open the heart.

Immediacy

Immediate experience is, in many ways, the most important touchstone of value in our culture. We seek to overcome barriers that stand between us and a recognition of our inner selves, the reality of those around us, participation in society, and contact with a natural world exceeding human powers. No idea can substitute for this experience.

I could not wait to attend this magical festival, and I was amazed that this style of trip was an all-expenses-paid extravaganza lasting two weeks in the USA. Mr Muscles and I had not been dating for very long, so I broke the news I was going abroad to him gently. But he was very liberal, and he wrapped his arms around me and whispered something surprising in my ear.

'I'll tell you what ... Why don't I give you a pink pass while you're at Burning Man?'

I looked at him quizzically. 'What's a pink pass?' I asked.

He laughed gently and said, 'It means you can do whatever you like with whomever you like, and you don't need to tell me about it.'

I was little taken aback. I didn't want to have to offer him a pink pass back as I was already battling feelings of jealously. Mr Muscles was so attractive, and he worked intimately with women, touching their bodies in classes and sessions.

I asked him if I could take some time to think about what he was suggesting, because I needed to take it in. It was the first time a boyfriend had been this liberal.

But the entire Burning Man trip was a dream come true. We started our trip in Las Vegas and Mr Party wanted us to learn. He was teaching us something so precious, and only someone in his position could take us out of our daily roles in order to be immersed in a philosophical life-lesson. That was what this was.

His first task was to show us a materialistic, money-orientated vacation experience so that we could appreciate the significance of the Burning Man values and community even more. I was with a clan of 10 of my colleagues and we all gathered on the main floor of a casino in the famous gambling capital.

'Everyone, I want you to think about this experience,' said Mr Party as he gathered us together. 'I am giving you $200 each, and I want you to spend it here on these gambling machines. I want you to not only notice how it feels spending the money, but also look at the faces and expressions of people around you. We will meet in a few hours to see how you find this experience.'

It was such an interesting activity, and my immediate reaction was that I didn't want to spend the money. I wanted to save it and spend it on something I would like to buy. The casino looked so boring and I didn't like the artificial atmosphere. However, I resisted my impulse and went and changed my money for chips. I began wandering the casino floor in order to start the experiment. Mr Party was right. People on the machines looked lifeless and lacklustre, mindlessly pushing the level of the pokie machines. Some looked like they had been sitting in the same position for hours. I noticed the environment was contrived, there were no timepieces anywhere, the lights were dimly lit, and it was easy to lose track of time. As I played the machines and tables, I didn't get any enjoyment from the aimless spending of money and I wasn't successful at winning. I could see what Mr Party wanted us to understand. Materialistic entertainment was a soulless endeavour.

We gathered that evening to discuss our experiences. Not everyone had found the night lifeless; it was interesting to get a team's feedback. Some people had won and come back with more than the $200 they began with; others had enjoyed the adrenaline and sportsmanship, but I couldn't wait for the next day when we would head to the Nevada Desert in an RV together.

We had two camper vans to house both teams and we all boarded in the morning, fresh from rest and excited for the trip ahead. I texted Mr Muscles while we still had signal, because once we reached the desert we would not be able to use our mobile phones. He texted back to wish me well and I knew he was still relaxed about the idea of me having a rendezvous. I didn't think I would take up the offer.

As we drove out of the cities the landscape rolled past and I gazed at the famous American outdoors. There were scenes I had seen on television but never in person – long rolling hills and vast canyons. It was awe-inspiring. We arrived, in the heat of the day, at the gates of Black Rock City. There was a crowd gathering, but the cars in the queue were not your average daily vehicles. Everyone had taken care to decorate their own, and there were people practising hula hoops or pois as they waited. Loud sound systems boomed from each vehicle.

Oh, I just loved the signs as we drove up to the gates. It felt as though I was being taken into a fantasy land and out of the default world. At last we reached the gates and found ourselves with The Greeters. The Greeters, like most staff at Burning Man, were volunteers. They were tasked with initiating all the camps and calling out the Burning Man virgins. As it happened, most of us were Burning Man virgins. We all had to perform an initiation to get through the gates. Mine was to kiss both Greeters on their cheeks and do a limbo-style backwards walk underneath a low bar to get to the other side. As I completed my task The Greeters gave me a huge hug and said two words that would resonate with me forevermore.

'Welcome home.'

Before I had even arrived, even as I was reading the 10 Burning Man Principles, I knew I was somewhere I would feel at home. The following seven days confirmed this. The atmosphere and cooperation, warmth and gift economy at Burning Man were just what I had been looking for.

The landscape of Burning Man is vast. It houses 50,000 people during the week of the festival, and it is the second biggest temporary city in the state of Nevada during its period of activation. There were enormous art sculptures towering into the sky, some two to three storeys high. I loved the phone booth. "Call God", it said. There were also letter installations with huge life-size words like L-O-V-E or O-I-N-K. This was a Disneyland for adults, but it was spurred on by the sense of community. I would explore more with each day. The principle of radical self-expression was in full effect. Everyone – and I mean everyone – was in a costume. This destination had attracted a huge population of like-minded revellers and highly creative artists. For the first time I wasn't the most crazily dressed person in the group. In fact, I didn't feel like I was an extrovert at all compared to these people. It was a revelation.

Camps of pirates roamed en masse. 'Ar har!' the leader swiped playfully at me with his mock cutlass. People were running up to me on the dancefloor to give me a befriending gift, like a friendship bracelet or keyring they had crafted. I was so touched. The atmosphere and the joy were palpable. Over the course of the week, the strength and closeness of this huge community became more evident. I had never seen such random acts of kindness or been invited by so many groups to take part in their camps, have a drink, or share a joke. I also liked the nudity and freedom to be topless or even walk fully naked without fear of being mocked or ostracised. This place was safe and free.

The main highlight was the night the Man would burn. The Man was a huge, towering effigy at the centre of the camp formation. The camp was well organised into a half-circle of streets and avenues, each stemming from a central point to the outer perimeter. We knew that on the night of "the burn" all the various sites would light bonfires and each group would gather for their local burning before converging together to watch the Man burn.

It was hedonistic and tribal. Fire dancers opened the ceremony around the Man; drummers beat drums in time with each other, adding electricity and anticipation to the atmosphere. We all hollered as the Man was lit. We cheered, and everyone danced with their friends and with strangers. People embraced.

I made life-long friends at that burning ritual, and I left a changed woman. I was a Burner through and through, and I made instant plans to return the following years. I had never really felt like I fitted within the conventions of modern society, but now I knew I wasn't alone. There were 50,000 like me out there and maybe more.

When I arrived back to England, Mr Muscles picked me up from Heathrow airport. He was the true romantic. As I reached the car I noticed that he had put a dozen red roses in the front seat to welcome me home. We embraced; it was so good to be in his arms again. And yet, there was still something that was not working between us. I tried to stifle it, but I couldn't. Mr Muscles had a natural charisma, and the fact that most of his clients were female left me distraught. In my mind they were all flirting with him, and my intuition told me I was unsafe. I was crippled with anxiety about this. I would feel terrible whenever another woman entered the room – my throat would constrict, and my heart would race. And so, one day I finally confessed all my worries to him in a flood of tears. Mr Muscles was amazing and gentle. He had actually been through therapy himself, so he kindly said he would accompany me if I wanted to get counselling.

I gave it a try, but I didn't get on with my counsellor. I really owe Mr Muscles a debt of gratitude for giving me the courage to take a step through the door to my own recovery, though. He encouraged me to open the door to the skeletons in my closet.

When the student is ready, the teacher arrives.

One day a pamphlet arrived in the mail. It had an unusual title that made me feel uneasy as I looked at it. The headline read *Liberate Your Sexuality* and it was a two-and-a-half-day weekend course. Mr Muscles put the brochure in front of me. 'Maybe we should go to this to work out our boundaries together,' he said.

I was so terrified. I knew I was being called to work on myself, to open up and confront the wounds of my past. It was terrifying, and I felt choked, but I drummed up the courage to call the number and enquired about how to register.

Mr Muscles and I were weeks away from moving to Australia. He had put the wheels in motion to get a job in Melbourne and had begun applying for a visa. I was conscious about spending money right before our big move, but I knew that this course could really help me – even though I didn't really know what it was all about.

To do the *Liberate Your Sexuality* course, I was required to attend the main course called the *More To Life Weekend* where I would be taught "the tools". It was essential that I understood these "tools" before I could do any other courses this organisation offered. I had to stay with a friend in London because the days were long; each day began at 8am and ended at 11pm. Mr Muscles was beaming at me as I packed my bags to go and do the first training course. He didn't need to come with me because he had already done the foundation course a few years earlier, and I was quietly relieved. I didn't know why I was paralysed with fear when he was around other women and it plagued me day and night. I wanted to be able to speak about it with people and not have him in the same room. Maybe they could help me.

'This is big stuff, Priscilla,' he said. 'You won't come back the same person. This will change you.'

One observation I will make about catching the train back into London is the number of signs that say, "Way Out". It is as if everyone who arrives in London is symbolically lost and looking to find an escape. People – tourists and residents alike – wander around the complex underground system faithfully following the Way Out signs. As I boarded the train at Waterloo to Covent Garden I wondered if I, too, would find my way out this weekend.

I felt stuck, like the needle of a record on a broken groove. I was frequently happy, carefree and joyous, yet occasionally this foreboding would infringe upon my serenity. I had tried to explore different counselling methods and even meditation techniques, but I could sense that there was another way out of this broken groove.

As I entered the room for the *More To Life* weekend I had to fill in my personal details, and the form asked if I had any pre-existing mental health issues. In hushed tones I explained to the registrars at the registration table that I had experienced a bipolar episode, and I was worried that whatever I was going to do on this course might trigger something or make me relapse. Although it had been seven years since my hospitalisation,

I was always cautious. I also still felt a deep shame about my breakdown and I didn't want it publicly known.

With kind eyes, the lady at the front desk explained it was absolutely fine. She told me to just relax and enjoy the day without giving it another thought but that I could speak to any of the team on hand if I needed help, and she would make sure the trainers also knew my medical history.

I walked into the room. It was pleasantly lit, with flowers decorating the front table and calming music. Other participants arrived; I counted at least 60 seats and slowly the room filled. I was on high alert, and a twinge of suspicion still tweaked at the back of my mind. What was this all really about?

At first, I'd thought that this looked suspiciously like a religious group. These people were too nice and too smiley. *I'll beat them at their own game,* I'd thought. *They're not going to be able to crack me.*

I did look further into it, though – I double and triple checked that it wasn't some religious mumbo jumbo. Mr Muscles swore there was nothing linked to religion whatsoever, and so did the lady who spoke to me when I called to enquire.

These feelings were familiar. I had always had a mistrust about some things, fearing that I might be walking back into a religious group. But now, as I walked into the room and saw everyone's friendly faces, I realised that there was nothing to fear. There was no judgement here. I was safe, and that was a huge relief.

At last it was starting time. Two women – the trainers – walked from the back of the room to the front down the middle aisles of the rows of seats. We all clapped as they made their entrance. They were very smartly dressed and had my full attention. They both stood next to neatly handwritten signs that had one word in capital letters. "NOTICE".

Notice what? I was so intrigued.

The first thing the two ladies did was ask us to pick up a sheet of paper we had been given. It had the word "Disciplines" across the top. Part of the training meant that we all had to commit to these disciplines. Could we all agree to do that?

We read them for a moment, and then people were allowed to ask questions. When all the questions had been asked, we stood and agreed to commit to the disciplines. I didn't realise how profound such a small set of tasks would prove to be. These all seemed easy enough; they were about timekeeping, being punctual, not having food or drink in the room and so on. I thought I would manage them easily! How wrong I was.

The trainers then drew a line across the top of a fresh sheet of paper and asked us all to name the emotions that we considered above the line – good emotions – and below the line – negative emotions. This was easy.

Over the course of the next two days I had the most profound wake-up call of my lifetime. I learnt why the original signs said "Notice". I was being reminded to notice my emotions, to notice when I was above and below the line. I had to make a diary to list events that changed me from one state to the other.

This was powerful.

Suddenly I was in control of my mind. It was not in control of me.

During each session we would learn new "tools". The best tool I found was called the "Clarity Process", and I still use it to this day. We then learnt an Authority Process, a Cost Process, Empowerment Conversation, Mirror Process and Disavow / Avow.

It was like a huge light bulb went on for me.

As we learnt the Cost Process, we were invited to make a list of all the people we had resented in our lives. We put it into two columns on the page. In the left-hand column was the name of anyone we resented. In the right-hand column was the number of years we had held on to that resentment. It could be a group of people or even an organisation. We were encouraged to get it all down.

I was shocked as I looked down my list.

• Mr Big

• DJ Digital

• Mr Condemnation

• DJ Shadow

• Mum

• Dad

• My sister

• Kid at primary school

• The DJ scene

• Christian Brethren

• The government

• The media

My list was so long – some of these resentments went back 15 years. I'd even had some of them for my whole life!

The lights were dimmed, and the music went on quietly. It was time to do the Forgiveness Process. I looked at my list and decided that the first and main person I wanted to forgive was my dad.

I followed the steps in my life tools handbook and I found a quiet place on the floor near the wall behind a screen. I took plenty of tissues.

The steps were like this:

Picture you are making eye contact with the person you want to forgive.

Tell them all that you have resented them for.

Tell them what the payoff has been.

Tell them what the cost has been.

Ask for forgiveness and offer them your forgiveness.

All around the room I could hear people break down in tears. My own tears were flowing and huge, heaving sobs burst from my chest. I resented Dad for burning my CDs and for being so rigid in my youth. I resented him for being so cautious with money, for being so practical, and always cautioning my crazy, creative outbursts. I realised that I had been justifying my resentment towards my dad with a payoff – the payoff was that I was right, that I was better than him, that I was the happier person and he was the miserable one. I would show him; I would rebel and prove myself.

I understood that my relationship with Dad had cost me my vulnerability. It cost us our closeness, as I was always defensive and ready to fight. As a result, I played out my rebellion all my life, in all sorts of destructive patterns with men including Mr Big, DJ Digital, DJ Shadow, and Mr Muscles. They had all been tarnished by remnants of the resentment I had towards my father. It was poisoning my relationships.

I cried my heart out.

A caring team member, a volunteer, came to hold my hand and gently support me. She helped me without words and with just the simple gesture of a fresh tissue. The simplicity of it and the depth of care made me cry even more.

I spent the whole weekend at the *More To Life* training bawling my eyes out. My mind and emotional landscape was like an untended garden overgrown with weeds. In order to get them out by the root, I needed to dig deeply to find the original cause. It was painful but worth it.

At the final session the room had such an incredible energy. There were smiles on the faces of all the participants. These smiles radiated from within them; they were not superficial. Someone told me that it looked like I had had a facelift because my eyes were so bright and my smile was so wide. I looked in the mirror. They were right!

This was it.

I was finding a way out of my thoughts and finding a clearer truth. I felt relieved and liberated. I couldn't wait to share this course with my family and loved ones. Above all, though, I knew the main person this material was would benefit was me. It was my calling to work with this. I chose to do it daily so I could shift my anxiety and move my life more towards to "above the line".

CHAPTER 8

SKYLINED

'The first step in self-fulfilment is to deal with your own negativity.'
K. Bradford Brown

Mr Muscles and I landed in Melbourne just before Christmas. We had packed a suitcase each and sent a shipping container full of our prized possessions, which would arrive by sea several months after we landed.

Something had shifted since I had done the *More To Life Weekend*, and the two of us had been propelled into a more connected relationship. We even sought couple's counselling to talk about my jealously issues. It was interesting to realise that both of us had had some abandonment issues related to a significant parent, and that this was triggering the behaviours we demonstrated when around the opposite sex. This was a profound step in our relationship, and we arrived into Melbourne closer than ever before.

The mistake I made was thinking it would be a good idea to live with my parents and save money. This was a disastrous idea, and it didn't help Mr Muscles to integrate into Melbourne life. We didn't have as much privacy as we had when we were living in our own flat. We had to remember little details about turning off the lights and how to use the internet. They were quite specific, and it hampered our freedom. My relationship with my parents was affected because I was unhappy and frustrated. I also felt I had lost a bit of my own identity coming back to Melbourne. I felt like a stranger in my hometown.

Mr Muscles had a job at his friend's studio, but he was homesick. I knew how he felt, remembering my homesickness when I arrived in London. He had also never been to Australia before, not even for a visit, so making Australia his permanent home was a huge adjustment.

I sympathised with his anxiety and I was saddened to see him sink into a depression of his own. We began hurriedly looking for our own home, but the damage had been done. Although his clients adored him, and he was joining athletics and cycling groups, he just couldn't settle, and he hit a wall. I felt so heartbroken. This happy-go-lucky guy – my hero, my knight in shining armour who had been the king of his hometown – suddenly changed into a shadow of his former glorious self. He became withdrawn. His smile no longer met his eyes. I was worried.

After we moved out and got our own place, he hit me with one sentence that sent me into a spiral of grief.

'I don't like it here, love,' he confessed with a heavy voice one evening. 'I'm really sorry but it's not for me. I'm going home to England.'

I was initially in shock. We had spent two years planning to migrate and he was one of the few English people who achieved a visa which was difficult to do yet he was throwing it all away. We had talked of marriage and babies. How could he do this to me?

He was right though. I was furious that he was throwing it all away, but I also wanted his happiness because he had shown such care when I had lived with him in his home. When my parents had visited England, he had given up his car so that we could take it to France. Instead he'd ridden a bike around town.

He'd even bought my mum a teapot as she loves proper tea. He got us all a special Q-Link health pendant to wear around our necks in order to balance energy. I wanted nothing more than for him to thrive.

I no longer thought about marriage in my future after he left. I resigned myself to healing the wounds and moving on.

I was relieved to finally be home and I didn't want to move back to England myself. It was hard to forge on ahead after parting with this person who had been an angel in my life. I wanted to show Mr Muscles the hospitality and care he had shown me when I moved to Surrey, so I moved out and lived in a friend's spare room. That way he could have our apartment until he shipped all his things back to England and flew back home.

I was grateful I had the *More To Life* training because it enabled me to use a lot of the tools straight away. I also enlisted a life coach to help me get through the grief. The grief was like a thick blanket over me, and I couldn't move it. I would wake up choked with tears. I lost my appetite. I was devastated and ashamed among my friends. I couldn't leave the house; I cried constantly, an unstoppable flood of tears.

Although I knew it was right to let him go, it still cut me to the core. I forced myself to go to the airport to watch him leave; I had to see him depart in order to let it sink in that he was really going, as painful as it was to watch him go. When he left I advertised the spare room and found a housemate.

After a few weeks with him gone, I made another major life decision. I had been employed by one of the world's leading music media companies, Myspace.com, and I was relishing my new day job. I had also resolved at the *More To Life* training that I was going to let my creativity flow. I even stood and made this declaration to the whole group at the end of the training.

It was like a penny had dropped. I realised that putting myself under pressure to write an instant hit song was hindering my creative inner child. The opportunities I'd had in the big studios in Italy had been ruined because I was "I must or else" on the song writing process. These kinds of demands meant I was creating anxiety for myself when I wanted to be in a free-flowing state to let ideas come naturally.

Something in me had switched off when I left London and moved back to Australia. It was as if I was giving up on the songwriting dream. I mean, I had Mr Muscles and I had a great career. I should have just been content to be at home and start a family! For a while I believed it; I believed I could actually shut off The Pull and be content. But the twinkling in my eyes had slowly begun to fade.

Trying to deny The Pull was unnatural and made me depressed. I knew this was my calling – it was almost a God-given gift. This natural ability to write songs and work with words and melodies isn't given to everybody. And so, when I tried to fit the comfortable mould that would make my parents feel at ease, I felt miserable inside. I was an actor, once again living a charade.

It was while I was working at Myspace that I got the itch to create my own profile and start networking online. At the time it was *the place* for online music profiles. Everyone had one. As I had the hit song with Audio Duo – who were now touring the world – I decided to put this online along with photos from my gig at Headquarters of House. I did this all with a quiet reserve and I really wasn't too fussed if I found collaborators or not. I was happy being back home with the sand, surf, and sun. I had missed the Southern Hemisphere summers. This online profile was just a tentative exploration.

Have you ever lost your car keys and looked in exasperation all over the house for them?

Have you found that the harder and harder you look, and the more exasperated you get, the less likely you are to find your car keys at all?

Have you also found that when you forget about the car keys and give up, something clicks? You slip back into the flow and hey presto, the keys show up without any effort at all!

Well, this next phase of my story was exactly like that.

I had given up on the idea of having a proper music career. I put feelers out online, but only tentatively. I was totally absorbed with my new job, which was exciting and involved working on a big music launch for the brand, too. I was letting my heart heal from the departure of Mr Muscles and I was distracted by all else that was going on. So, can you imagine my surprise when my online profile got a "like" from a group of music producers in Bristol in the UK? Imagine further my surprise when I read their online message: *You have a great voice, Priscilla. We'd love to write with you.*

I nearly fell off my seat!

I also laughed to myself. Was this the cosmic joke? I had just left England and come all the way back to Australia, and now these guys were finally contacting me. Why was this happening? It seemed unreal.

I also had begun teaching burlesque classes in Melbourne and I discovered to my delight that burlesque was still relatively undeveloped as a scene in my hometown, whereas in London it had become oversaturated and mainstream. One of the gyms I was teaching at loved my class ideas; the director called me and said, 'We would love to put your classes into six of our gyms. Our members have been asking for burlesque.'

Naturally I agreed, and I was delighted to get the support of a major chain that was respected in the fitness industry.

My media and advertising background held me in good stead and I sent the gym a range of photos from my London burlesque shows, which they could use for promotion. So then, when I arrived to teach at the first gym, I turned up at the entrance and was stunned. My face was all over huge posters in the stairwell and main reception. I had a faint flicker of anxiety when I arrived to teach the classes. I noticed I was "below the line". I was becoming more attuned to the effects my emotions had on my body. I felt the anxiety in my heart when I saw my face on the poster. I could feel tension in my jaw. My breath became more and more shallow. I was able to separate from myself in the moment and look down into the scenario, as if I was an actor in a scene.

Could I live up to this? What if I was a huge a disappointment?

I later sat down with my processing book. The processing book was one of the tools I had adopted since the *More To Life* training. It was like a journal, and I would keep a list of any events throughout my day that changed my emotional state for the better or for the worse. Some of life's events would be very positive and bring me great happiness, and I wanted to make sure I captured all of those, too.

As I looked at this current life event – seeing my huge face on large posters at the gym – I realised it was activating a core belief I held about myself. I wrote out all the thoughts I had when I saw my photo on the posters in my processing book. There was a separate line for each thought.

The immediate emotion I felt was fear.

The place I felt that fear was in my heart; it made my chest tighten up.

As I had learnt to do in the *More To Life* training, I closed my eyes and went back to the moment I saw my face on the posters. I began some stream-of-consciousness writing.

- *My face is on a huge poster*
- *There is an expectation on me now*
- *I must not mess this up*
- *I have to be the best*
- *I must have an amazing class or else ...*
- *Or else I will be a huge disappointment*

• *And if I am a huge disappointment*
• *Basically, I am ... not good enough.*

I was amazed at what the negative core belief was. It boiled down to one simple statement: "I am not good enough".

It was interesting because this negative core belief kept coming up to haunt me. I had noticed it was underlying a lot of my jealousy issues with Mr Muscles and now it was back in a different form. What was also interesting to observe was that I was scared if I failed and scared if I succeeded. The fear came at me from both sides of my goal. What a strange catch-22! I was setting myself up for anxiety no matter which way I achieved it.

Feel the fear and do it anyway, I told myself.

I decided to use the Avow/Disavow process on a daily basis. I would spend 10 minutes shaking my whole body, telling myself that it was a lie that I wasn't good enough. This was the disavow. I would say this over and over again, and then state the avow. It came to me naturally after the solid disavow, and it was beautifully succinct: "I am enough."

For the avow I would put on uplifting orchestral music and stand straight up with my feet planted and my hands raised in the air.

'I am enough ... I AM enough ... I am enough ...'

As these words sank into my psyche, tears sprang to my eyes. How long had I been punishing myself for not being enough? The truth is, I was! I was perfect. I was enough.

It was a huge revelation.

This was the beginning of sowing the right mental seeds and re-landscaping my inner garden. I was weeding out the negative core beliefs and planting the new positive affirmations. Each day I did this I felt something shift.

I was like the butterfly leaving her pupa. The new me was waiting to emerge.

*

The burlesque classes were taking off, and with my new positive rituals I was getting bolder in following my passions. There were just too many positive signs to ignore, too many indications that I could have another life and income outside the world I had always known as an employee. I had the team of producers in Bristol ready to release a new track of mine, I had two of Australia's most famous songwriting twins, Nervo, contacting me via my online music profile, and I had my classes in six locations. These were all omens.

So I decided to take a leap of faith. I quit my day job and committed, for the first time, to completely follow The Pull. I was going to be a full-time artist and business owner.

I had managed to save enough money while living in London to have a deposit for a house, and although I was approved for a mortgage, I decided to throw caution to the wind and follow my heart. All the signs seemed to be leading me to this decision and doors were opening that had never opened before. I reckoned to myself that I would pretend I was on a working holiday for a year, and if it really did not work out, then a year later I would apply for a job and commence my career in the corporate world again.

It was yet another level of personal reclamation and lifestyle transformation.

Sapphira's Showgirls was born.

Butterflies became the mascot of my dance school. I gave one to each student who arrived to begin classes with me, and it was lovely to sit the group in a circle and welcome each student with a small gift. I wanted to nurture each individual and help them bring about their own awakening. I began planning a student showcase, because for me, the act of performing and being seen by friends and family was the final stage of the full transformational evolution. I sourced a local bar and all of us began to eagerly await the showcase day.

To really establish myself as a new business, I knew I needed to enlist a designer and I put my feelers out within my network in the creative community. To my surprise, London popped back into view, as a friend suggested working with a designer she knew in Battersea.

What was it with this British city? Would I ever escape?

It was funny connecting via Skype with this new designer. Our regular sessions soon became nicknamed Sky-Type as we would connect online every morning and night. I had an immediate attraction to this new designer – we'll call him The Captain. He would sign off his emails with "Sent from my iPhonium" and this made me giggle. I liked his sense of humour.

In Bristol, my lyrics were becoming more developed. I was thrilled when the original crew connected me with another key music producer in their team. I'll call him Bee-Loved. Bee-Loved had owned a music studio for 15 years and loved my voice, so we also began to have daily Skype calls in the morning and night. I was in overdrive. Songs were pouring out of me. I made 23 songs in quick succession, but also I had a laptop and synthesiser. I was learning about midi and music was flowing. I was now empowered because I could record my own voice and create the background structure with loops and chords to showcase the style of my songs. This meant I could send music anywhere without having to carry an upright piano with me to play my music. Such convenience!

Bee-Loved and The Captain became two significant co-creators. Both of them naturally seemed to find the images and sounds to develop my own ideas without any discussion needing to take place. This was a beautiful and spiritual connection; it was deep and profound. I decided I needed to meet them both, and so you can imagine the quiet chuckle I had with myself as I found myself logging on the internet to book a flight.

I was going back.

Back to the scene of the crime.

Back to London.

Back to follow The Pull.

Back to chase my dream.

CHAPTER 9

ONE LOVE

'I see you in art
I hear you in music
I see you
And I find myself'

Mirror Image, Sapphira

I have always likened finding someone who understands you musically to be akin to finding the person you want to marry. There needs to be a level of spiritual connection for that individual to decipher the tone, nuance, and message of a song. I didn't realise how complex and difficult it would be finding that very special someone. I only knew how much it offended my ears when that connection was not there. I would occasionally hear back from producers whose translation of my work caused me great upset. The use of my voice, their rearrangement of lyrics or – even worse – omission of key lines and chord progressions not only grated on my nerves but seemed like a deep insult, because it demonstrated the disconnection instantly. If they could not write music to complement my musicianship in a way that worked, there could be no collaboration. Partnership was falling at the first hurdle.

I also was unaware how provocative and intimate it would be to find someone who did mirror the essence of my soul through music. As I began daily Skype sessions with Bee-Loved, something glorious began to emerge.

I have mentioned that I could listen to accents for hours and never get bored. There is a seductive musicality itself in the way the tongue rolls around the lips and teeth while forming words. In particular, I melt at the sound of male English accents, and without a doubt the tone of someone's voice and command of vocabulary are as great an aphrodisiac to me as candlelight, champagne, and a hotel suite (but I'll happily take one or all of them any day, by the way).

Mr Big had a deep and commanding boom to his London accent. The Captain had a soft, husky British tone. Dr Flame had a firm elocution like a stern headmaster. But Bee-Loved … Bee-Loved's voice poured over me like warm swathes of honey. Every sharp pronunciation, every clipped word of English slang with the sexy indifference of dropped syllables like "qual'ty" and "prodooocer" sent shivers down my spine. Bee-Loved was living in Bristol, where he had been based for 20 years. He told me lots of stories about the music industry and managing a studio in Redland. I marvelled at the fact that we were only meeting now long-distance as I was stuck back in Melbourne. Just a year ago I had been a short train ride from Paddington to the West Country. Now I was a 24-hour flight away from dear old Blighty.

Little did I know, during these precious moments of early acquaintance, that I was entering the Holy of Holies. This was it – the most divine rite of passage for any songwriter, a moment that happens to very few. I was meeting my musical equal, my twin flame, my soulmate. My one true love.

I felt like my wings were spreading so that my spirit could fly. Transformation.

As a matter of course, Bee-Loved and I talked about everything. Some of our calls would last for four hours. Due to the time difference between the Northern and Southern Hemispheres, I would wake to hear his voice in the morning as he was settling for bed and call him just before bedtime as he was waking up. We talked every day, so naturally we began discussing the opposite sex. When we discovered we were both going through a recent break-up, we consoled one another. I had had a rare phone call from Mr Muscles who was back in Surrey now, and Bee-Loved told me he was going through a divorce. He sounded so heartbroken when he talked about his marriage ending. I was touched by his obvious sensitivity, and he was a very gentle and caring soul. Each day we got to know each other better; I loved the discourse and our shared love of music. Bee-Loved's music was phenomenal – he embellished my songs in a way I had being longing for, but I'd given up hope that it would ever happen.

He was also a pianist and had taught himself bass, guitar, and drums. I realise now why this enriches his music. He has an affinity with every layer of sound he replicates through software production. Every morning I would log on to my computer, eager to see if a new file had been uploaded so I could listen to how our music was progressing. It was a mutual fixation, and he and I were both heavily into a long-distance collaboration. It was bordering on obsession.

The most beautiful communication between two humans is unspoken. Bee-Loved and I shared an unspoken bond. And despite all the miles of distance between us and all the years of experience we both had, we had one particular thing in common.

Bee-Loved had also once been part of the Brethren Church.

This arose early in conversation when Bee-Loved commented on a lyrical phrase I was using with Biblical reference. 'Yes, I was raised in a Brethren Church community,' I offered in hushed tones. Even uttering the words left a bitter taste swirling in my mouth. But when I learnt that Bee-Loved had also been tarnished by his experience, we both let out a sigh of relief. Here was someone who understood me.

I explained my breakdown and psychosis. He wasn't surprised; he could see how the pressures of that life could have created undue stress, especially on a young artist. He, too, had been admonished by elders at his church for playing guitar and writing rock music. We both bore the scars. There was a comfort in this shared experience that I cannot articulate to the uninitiated. It was reassuring and uplifting.

I felt Bee-Loved was sent as part of my musical evolution. I also felt like he was there to heal my old church wounds, too. I have never been more grateful for the way his music has helped me find my voice.

As I had recorded several of my songs a cappella, our initial excursions in the land of music were one directional. I sent him my ideas and he wrote around them. One day he asked if we could try something new. I was totally open to any suggestions and I couldn't believe that at last I had a music producer on speed dial who wanted to work with me. This had taken seven years to happen, so I was overjoyed. Of course we could try something different, I told Bee-Loved. He had a track he had written; he wanted to send it to me to see if I could create a song over the top of it – a top line, as it's known in the biz. I said yes, but I was anxious. I had written in this way before and it had always been a blow to my confidence because I never heard back from the studio. The radio silence weighed heavily on my mind. What was I doing wrong? What wasn't I hearing? What did they want? It made me angry – angry at myself and angry at them. It spurred me on to take composition into my own hands, and in later years I would learn studio skills of my own so that I could shape sounds and percussion around my songs the way I wanted to.

I used to pester Mr Big so much. 'Why?' I would quiz him miserably. 'Why would they ask me to write something and then never come back to me? It's so mean.'

'It just doesn't suit their direction,' Mr Big would reassure me gently. 'Don't take it too personally.'

I was terrified this might happen yet again with Bee-Loved, and I didn't want to upset the flow of something that I felt was going so well. *Feel the fear and do it anyway,* I lectured myself quietly.

He sent me his track and I downloaded it and put it on my phone. It was a powerful piece; the beats and bassline were aggressive, and I could feel his energy and essence between the tones. There was so much chemistry already between us on the phone that this music began exuding something private and illicit within me. I went to my studio I flicked on the microphone and plugged in the headphones. This was when I found her.

She wasn't Sapphira. There was a different layer to this alter ego. Buried beneath the pristine sheen of the superficial showgirl was a twisted, more sinister character. And she was pissed off.

All those years of being supressed and ashamed of my own sexuality suddenly whirled up inside me with an unstoppable force.

My eyes narrowed to fine slits.

My fingernails curled.

My fingers glided up the microphone stand and gripped the sharp, cool metal around the shaft of the microphone.

I opened my mouth and growled ominously.

'Sweet child
You've been a bad boy
Your mother told you
Don't play with fire ...'

The rest of the song, which later became 'Hide & Seek' by Sapphira and Tonestepa, wrote itself, but this new energy in me was being evoked by Bee-Loved and the beats within his music. I was a different woman. I tilted my head back and sexual throaty groans came out of my mouth. I panted. I didn't know who this was or where she was coming from, but I was not at liberty to refuse her. When she was finished, when it was done, I fell back onto my mattress in the studio, exhausted. I ended the recording and uploaded the file to send to him.

It was different this time. I didn't feel anxious about whether he would like it or not. I knew this was good and I was eager to hear his reaction. We were making music; we were recording sex.

As I made the journey back to London, I had a wry smile on my face. I had packed my bags seven years ago and left Melbourne to take over the music scene and commence my path to glory. I had returned, dejected. Yet here I was again, triumphantly going back to meet a team of music producers – and, in particular, my main writing partner, Bee-Loved.

I listened to the songs that we had been working on through my headphones. We had 14 tracks altogether; it had been a rapid and long-distance explosion of ideas. I had also created the space in my life by being able to concentrate full-time on music and teaching dance classes. I was a free spirit, and I was surrounding myself with books on creativity and joining artist meet-ups, too.

I was on personal development overdrive. I was hungry for more life learning. I enrolled in all the *More To Life* courses I could. I had decided to fly to New Zealand to complete *Making Money Count* and to retake the original *More To Life Weekend*, this time with my mother. After seeing Bee-Loved in London, I was going to Giggleswick in Leeds to be part of a seven-day residential *More To Life* course, *Way of a Warrior*. I also sponsored Bee-Loved to do the course, too. I knew if we both could be more alert to our triggers and emotions, it would enhance our communication and business collaboration.

Now at a layover at Hong Kong airport, I looked out the windows while listening to my iPod. I wondered what it would be like to meet Bee-Loved in person. There was so little material about him online – and believe me, I had done more than the routine level of stalking to see if I could unearth any pictures – but he was a recluse and camera shy. He was aggravatingly private. My internet searches were coming up blank. Only a few times had he put on his webcam so we could chat face-to-face. Mostly the calls worked better with just audio, so really we had been getting to know each other the old fashioned way with Skype calls, emails and the occasional written letters.

When I arrived into London I went directly to my sister's house. She had relocated to England's capital after I had left the city, but it was positive because it meant I had a base and another good reason to go back and visit. I had planned to see Bee-Loved a week later by catching a train to Bristol, but when I arrived at my sister's my curiosity got the better of me.

I pulled out my mobile phone to place the call.

Ring, ring.

Ring, ring.

It felt strange to hear the difference on the phoneline in comparison to the Skype call. I was now in the same time zone as Bee-Loved, this mystery man, and we would soon be in the same room.

When he answered I urged him to come to London that afternoon. 'I'm too impatient to wait to see you,' I declared. 'Let's meet up today.'

It's amazing how some places pull us back time and time again. Bee-Loved's train would be pulling into Paddington and we agreed that he would catch a train to meet me at The Spot.

As I waited for him nervously, I imagined what we might look like from a radar screen. I imagined our heartbeats showing as two pulsating lights, glowing that bit brighter as they moved closer together, close to converging in one place for the first time.

Full circle.

Only metres from where I had first met Mr Big – and later heard 'Circles' with Audio Duo – the third incredible step in my music career was about to take place. My principal music producer was about to arrive.

I thought carefully about what to wear; I wanted to create the right impression. I decided on a demure top, cream with an elegant bow on the side. I paired it with a suit jacket and jeans. I also was eager that we keep our relationship strictly professional, despite our flirtations and the sexual content of our music. There was too much at stake to muddy the water with a fling.

'You shouldn't get involved with people you write with,' Mr Big had often knowingly advised me. 'You lose more than you do in a normal relationship. You lose your art.'

I planned on following his advice. Honestly, I did. It's just that reality and sensibility were about to take a total departure from my logical mind.

It took a little coordination to find each other, but when at last I turned a corner, I could see the outline of a towering masculine figure. It matched the shape and contours of the few photos I had found. This was he.

'Bee-Loved?' I called, walking up behind him.

When he turned to look at me, it was as though there was a visible spark. There was a sizzle. I could feel the crackle of electricity – I felt it on every level. My skin, my heart, my head, my eyes – they were all on fire.

'Hello, darling,' he said with a huge smile. We both grinned from ear to ear and he swept me up in a huge bear hug.

I breathed him in. After only eight months of connecting solely with our voices, it was a significant moment to be here together in person. I shook my head and stepped back, dusting off my jacket. *God, Priscilla, keep it professional,* I thought. My mind was wandering into all the forbidden places.

We went for a walk to share some lunch. Keeping it professional lasted only for two hours. I invited him back to my hotel room.

And the rest, as they say, is history.

CHAPTER 10

WHAT WOULD DITA DO?

'Look at you, representing Australia.'
Dita Von Teese

I have mentioned that I am a cyclist, and I have always loved this nifty mode of transport. I advocate practicality. Call me the eco-ecdysiast. So if I can ride, I will. And of course, this is much to the hilarity of onlookers and passers-by. You can imagine my embarrassment when, as I press on the brakes at traffic lights, sometimes my overloaded pannier bags discard dazzling sequinned shoes or shiny outfits. It isn't easy to dismount, retrieve said shiny escapee, and remount in the space of time it takes for the lights to flash from red to green. The speeds at which I have mastered costume retrieval warrant making the act an Olympic sport.

The security gates at the airport have always been an interesting experience. Of course, feather fans seem to come up quite clearly on the security airport scans, and I have had many embarrassing moments explaining to airport staff why I need a special carry-on bag for my feather headdresses, which will be damaged if transported in any kind of hold luggage. I have even worn my headdress through the baggage checks to avoid paying extra fees, as you do!

To reduce the weight of my carry-on luggage I also once put on all my underwear, four bras, suspender belts and a girdle with a loose summer dress over the top. Can you imagine my horror when, as I went through the body scan at the airport, the metal underwire in the bras kept going off? Naturally, as the female security guard pulled me to one side to pat over my clothing, she raised an eyebrow after feeling a very lumpy bodice underneath. 'I'm sorry, Ma'am. I am going to have to ask you to step to one side with a colleague of mine to complete a strip search,' she said.

Yes. As we went into the airport security room, I had to lift up my dress to reveal all my layers of underwear and swimsuits. 'Are you sure you're not hot with all that on, love?' The airport guards creased over in peals of laughter.

'Yes, I'm fine,' I sighed. 'You know what's even funnier though, ladies? I am a burlesque artist and this is giving a lot of ideas for a new act.'

I'd like to think I got the last laugh, but I'm not sure I did.

False eyelashes ... What a mystery. We have never got along. It seems to be just my luck that as I am sitting patiently with my eyes closed, allowing that darn glue to set, I get called to perform moments too early and my eyes won't open because I have glued them together.

While I may have the sexiest jewel-adorned underwear, you can rest assured that you'll find a far less sexy sock sewn into the insides at the back to secure my electronic equipment. It's a needs-must affair, my dears! I learnt quickly that the battery pack for my microphone has to be secured in a pocket in my underpants during my first tassel twirling performance in Lincolnshire. It was going well until – when bouncing up and down – I felt the cold sensation of a mic wire trickling down my legs. Like an umbilical cord, the battery pack of my headset microphone had dislodged and was now dangling between my thighs, hitting the floor with a clattering thud. I had given birth to a virtual battery pack!

Pure class, I tell you!

One of the world's most prevalent burlesque artists spearheading the burlesque revival is known all over the globe by her stage name, Dita Von Teese. And it is during the course of my many guerrilla changing room extravaganzas that I have murmured, sighed, cursed, and – depending on the severity of the crisis I am handling – even shouted, 'What would Dita $%£&(*$&56£% do?!'

She is renowned for her commitment to advocating glamour, but above all she has been a powerhouse and has a prolific commercial ability to open up the burlesque scene with her exceptional performances and polished shows. This has enabled major brands to align with the artform. Indeed, I tip my hat to her for helping the dance reach a mainstream audience and helping it to become respected and revered. She, too, is so respectable.

It was an honour to meet Dita in person when I was first putting out my feelers as a young artist. She was making an appearance at a book signing in London's West End. Her book, *Burlesque and The Art of The Teese*, became a big inspiration for me, and it was incredible to have a personal dedication written in her delicate handwriting on the front page. What I loved most about the book was that it echoed what I was finding in my own craft. One side showed Dita as the glorious showgirl personified, but when you flipped the book and turned it upside down, you saw Dita's darker fetish personality, too. This was where my own exploration began. I was noticing that I, too, had a darker tendency as an artist. It was as if Sapphira had an alter ego herself. Seeing this visual affirmation of the duality within the one performer gave me the courage to explore my own darkest imaginings, too.

Dita's courageous leadership as a burlesque role model encouraged me. Discarding my employment and following my heart took a lot of willpower, and I knew she had been similarly brave. Setting up any business and becoming an entrepreneur is fraught with risks.

Dita had reached the fulfilment of her own self-expression, which was evident in her shows and costuming. I knew I was on the same journey, but I was still a pupa in the chrysalis.

When the Brethren indoctrination raised its voice inside my head – and when I pictured the disapproving frowns of Mr Condemnation and others who had excommunicated me – I would feel discouraged. It deterred me from my evolution. And yet there was Dita, shining a light. She was a fearless leader, a pioneer, the evolved embodiment of erotica. With her example I forged on ahead, despite the inner demons of self-doubt frequently surfacing to plaguing me.

I would only realise later how significant my first meeting with her was, especially as I went on to start my own company championing women's self-expression.

Being a self-actualised sensual being brings out the light and the shadows in other women around us.

There have been many instances throughout my career when I have often paused to think to myself: *What would Dita do?* I've marvelled at her careful poise and disposition and compared it with my own. There are so many mishaps that occur during the course of being a live performance artist, so it's impossible not to be in awe of our burlesque queen's decorum.

I have had to be a practical burlesque performer, given the nature of my modest profile. There are very few of us who have a creative team travelling with us; often we are on our own or we enlist the support of friends or relatives. Even fewer of us command the kind of fee that includes road transport, such as a taxi to and from the venue. I always think it's a mark of a relationship when someone agrees to wheel my wheelie suitcase on public transport, so I don't have to arrive at a show feeling sweaty and flustered. Very kind souls, indeed!

I've come to realise that behind burlesque is a massive support network, a cottage industry of helpful volunteers and family. The scene would not survive without these people, and

I am so eternally grateful for all those who have helped me. It amounts to a small army, so I can only image how much further that network extends across the globe.

Thank you to each and every one of you!

*

Picture the most stylish streets on a Parisian afternoon. The Champs-Élysées, the Notre-Dame.

I am in Paris to see Dita's show at a famous cabaret club. The sex shops along the Boulevard de Clichy near the Moulin Rouge beckon me to enter.

Some boutiques are curated to perfection. They have immaculately groomed attendees, soft light settings and furnishings. As I'm in Paris to see Dita's Crazy Show at Le Crazy Horse, I reason I should commemorate the occasion with some new underwear. When in Rome, do as the Romans do. When in Paris, do what Dita does!

I find myself in an unfortunately less manicured boutique that has gorgeous garments at half the price of the designer stores. The shop assistant here is a balding older man who barely seems to speak any English. I feel awkward asking for his assistance in matters of little lacy lady things. I have some lingerie on hangers that I wish to try, so instead I hold up the delicate items and gesture to ask if there is a changing room. With a heavy hand, he pushes me towards a flimsy makeshift construction where a white sheet is balanced on some rickety elastic. I am unsure, but as it seems there is no alternative I decide to don the garments regardless. Trying feebly to close the gap in the white sheet to preserve my modesty proves pointless, because as I bend to remove my clothing the folds of the sheet keep opening wide and showing the whole store my predicament and, unfortunately, my shiny pale derrière.

At last I wrestle the two sheets together and fasten them with my hair clip. Now to contend with the underwear. I notice that the tag says, in English, "shapewear". Why yes, this is what I need. This figure-hugging corset snakes over my breasts like a tube and squeezes my stomach and hips into obedience with tight metal boning and elastic. I am impressed. I turn side to side, but there is little room in the changing area. I decide I want to buy this; I've never felt so svelte with such a flat tummy. Divine, darlings!

This is when disaster strikes.

As I lift the bottom of the shapewear girdle to pull the corset over my head, I get stuck. I am now butt naked from the waist down, with my arms pinioned over my head. I can't bend my arm and I can't see. My face is covered by this shape-forming elastic, but it is so skin-tight I can't get out. My arms flop helplessly from side to side. My bum and muff are exposed. How can I call back the balding shop assistant for help?

This is too embarrassing. I begin to panic, and this does little to improve the situation. 'Fuck! Fuck!'

I stop and reason with myself. *Be quiet. Breathe. The only way out of this is to breathe,* I tell myself. I stand still, arms strapped above my head and my eyes covered. In a haze of darkness, I find a place of tranquillity for a brief respite. *This mindfulness stuff really comes in handy,* I think glibly. With several deep breaths and controlled movement, I slowly find a way to unhinge myself. I finally escape the underwear from hell.

I still buy it. Nothing has ever made my stomach that flat.

Later that night, Dita effortlessly preens on stage with a bathtub faucet. I sigh to myself. If she could master her plumbing props on stage, could she ever get stuck in shapewear in a downtown Parisian lingerie store? If she was pinioned by her own underwear, what would happen? What would she do?

As I wistfully admire her limitless poise from afar, the realisation dawns on me that such a crisis would never happen to a woman like her.

I am in a uniquely wonky world of my own.

CHAPTER 11

MY HEART BELONGS TO BRANSON

'I love challenging myself, I love doing things people think
are impossible, and I love breaking records.'
Sir Richard Branson – virgin.com

My time in London with Bee-Loved and my sister was soon over.
I wistfully departed for Australian shores, feeling the familiar
tug on my heartstrings. My home was in two distant places. The
bittersweet divide had haunted me for years. I thought of my
early phone calls with my family and nan in England, and then
about my more recent sparks with Mr Big and Mr Muscles. Now
I had to leave my second base and return to my birth country.

It never gets easier. I leave a piece of me behind permanently
each time, but I have grown accustomed to the dull ache. It is part
of my life's tapestry. I have chosen to travel, and my heartstrings
have reached far and wide. But it still means that at some point in
the world I am separated from people I cherish dearly.

Bee-Loved and I commenced regular Skype sessions again. He
was smitten and wanted to move to Australia. But I was jittery.

Remnants of the anguish I felt at Mr Muscles' departure had left me with harrowing memories.

'Can you endure it all again?' my best friend Boo Boo asked me.

I knew I couldn't, so I tried to block Bee-Loved out of my mind. The possibility of him living in Australia seemed impossible, and the immigration process is not for the faint-hearted. I wasn't sure our blossoming musical partnership would survive such an upheaval, so I told Bee-Loved that we must continue on professionally and find people in our local areas to date.

It was an unfortunate twist when Mr Bee-Loved got engaged to a jealous ex-girlfriend a few months later, and she forbade him any contact with me. For a year and a half I lost contact with my soulmate. I also lost all my files and all my work. I felt like someone had kidnapped my babies but there was nothing I could do to get the communication flowing. Mr Big appeared as an apparition in my mind, with his words of wisdom about not getting involved with business partners. I knew he had been right, but I didn't know what I could do.

I threw myself into my dance class business, and I was pleased to be unearthing some starlets in my classes. I approached these core girls and asked if they would like to create a troupe. Each of them could perform a solo and I would choreograph the group routines, creating a show with a combination of performances. It was so much fun, and they all flourished. I flourished too. It was great having a cosy creative coven.

Occasionally we would be tutored by a male choreographer, and we also had a male soloist join our group. But principally it was a girl gang, and it was brilliant. It was during the height of our success in Melbourne that I hatched a plan: we should take our show to London. Ultimately, I wanted to bolster each of my students' confidence by showing them that not only could we sell out shows in Melbourne, but they could also see their names on posters across Soho, a famous cabaret theatre district of

London's West End. It was a self-esteem enhancement exercise for them, but little did I know how character building it would be for me too. It was also a huge amount of work, because we needed to raise the funds for our flights.

It just so happened that my beloved Boo Boo had moved to England. Her family had been relocated for a work position, so she warmly opened her home to accommodate us. This was perfect – we now just needed to worry about the flights and booking venues.

At the corner of my mind was the image of a shaggy, blonde-haired renegade who I knew owned an airline. His name was Sir Richard Branson. His airline had done a major publicity stunt, painting a burlesque artist on the side of an aircraft. As I knew about branding, I knew this airline would understand the aesthetic of burlesque. Perhaps we could reach out in a unique way to get sponsorship and support.

Thus, an idea was formed.

Initially it was only a flicker at the recesses of my mind, but soon it would engulf my world and my life.

In my regular shows I would change the lyrics of 'My Heart Belongs to Daddy' and substitute the word "daddy" with the name of an audience member. Sometimes it would be 'My Heart Belongs to David.' I even had 'My Heart Belongs to Jurgen' and 'My Heart Belongs to Hymen' ... you never knew which names you would get at a burlesque show! It always got the audience laughing.

I decided to change the lyrics to the song and form an online plea to Virgin. I wanted the flights to be donated to us. 'My Heart Belongs to Branson' seemed to roll off the tongue, and before too long we enlisted a film maker to help us create the video in key locations around Melbourne.

It was a fun day making the video. I have never seen so many smartphones held out to record our group. I wonder if tourists have some of that footage on their phones that we have never seen. When the director sent through the final edit, I loved it. But the next part was going to be a little harder. How on Earth would we reach this esteemed businessman? I knew our video was good, but I was sure he would get approached by people all the time.

I decided to put an announcement online that I was looking for a publicist. When Madame PR replied to my message, I had another nearly-falling-off-my-seat moment. Madame PR was one of the most famous publicists in Melbourne. The weighty list of personalities who had engaged her services was star-studded; it practically twinkled from the pages of her surreptitious website.

Could Madame PR really want to represent little ol' me?

In a few short emails, we arranged to meet at Rendezvous, a swanky spot near her home. I was flustered in preparation.

And, of course, as luck would have it, my car broke down the day before our meeting.

So I resorted to my favourite mode of transport.

The venue wasn't far from my home.

I could do this by bicycle.

Eco-ecdysiast, ignite!

The next morning, I was up early and I planned my trip carefully. I needed plenty of time to arrive at Rendezvous, as I planned to hide my bike around the corner. Also, my bike helmet left a welt across the right side of my scalp, and I hoped that if I arrived early enough it would disappear before Madame PR got there. Or I could cover it with foundation.

What would Dita do? Not arrive at a meeting with Madame PR with a bike helmet welt!

See, I can advocate glamour too!

Fake it till you make it, I told myself.

When Madame PR entered the restaurant, she glided in with a confidence and brashness I couldn't help but admire. I was intrigued by her enigmatic presence, and our conversation flowed easily from the first hello. In a matter of a few minutes, I felt like we had known each other for our entire lives. I felt totally secure entrusting her with my wild idea.

'I want to ask Sir Richard Branson to be my Valentine,' I said cheekily. 'We want to take our show, Burlesque or Bust, to London. I hope to get flights.'

And then Madame PR pulled me close to her and whispered conspiratorially, 'I know how to reach him. Leave it with me.'

We planned to launch the story on Valentine's Day. I combined her PR network with my own – she could tackle the major press outlets and I would contact local papers and specialist titles. It was a giddy moment, and the whole group was on tenterhooks waiting for Valentine's Day to roll around. The press release went out across the media channels and I was delighted to see that we got the attention of some major journalists.

The biggest victory occurred the next day.

I don't know why I was anticipating that it would take a week to get a reply, but it didn't. The day after our video was released, I received a direct email from Madame PR's source.

Sir Richard is delighted with your video. He sends his love back. I was grinning from ear to ear. We were only offered a discount – I was offered vouchers – and not the full price of the flights, but I was still delighted. Within weeks we had got the support of a major corporate company, along with permission to use their logo on our flyers. I thought we were set.

Another interesting collaboration was about to curve into view. I had been teaching burlesque classes in a prestigious area. A gorgeous woman, Miss Pristine, was also a teacher, and she was a huge encouragement in my career. She would often pop up with CDs to give me inspiration for my music and she occasionally introduced me to photographers, too, as she had been a performer herself. When Miss Pristine called me with an offer, she told me it was the chance of my career. 'There is an artist painter in town. He needs someone to pose for a picture for him, possibly as a nude. But look him up; he is very reputable, and most people would clamber at the chance to model for him.'

The artist's name was Billich. I had never posed nude before, but I agreed to sing and pose in exchange for a fee. Along I went with wonder at what lay in store.

Prior to the sitting I had the inspiration to get my make-up done. I had discovered a fantastic company specialising in theatrical make-up, and I thought that if I had to be sprawled out stark naked on a table, at least a few strokes of eyeshadow and some fake eyelashes would give me some armour with which to face the outside world. It's all about keeping up appearances, sweeties!

Adorned with make-up and with a long, Godiva-inspired wig in my bag, I headed to the gallery. When I met Billich he introduced himself by his first name, Charles. I gave him a butterfly, as was my custom. I think there must be hundreds of thousands of butterflies sparkling on fridges and noticeboards in homes across the world, all bestowed as a token of gratitude from me. Charles was so pleasant and amenable. He pinned his butterfly to his lapel and I went nervously backstage to change.

Well, to undress.

The marble table I was to lie on looked cold, but it was the least of my worries. I was conscious that I had a mosquito bite that was turning into a bright shining welt on my bum. I hoped there would not be anybody positioned at the back of the room.

I had asked prior to our meeting for there to be no cameras, but this is the modern age. As I commenced my first position, I couldn't very well gesture rudely to the patrons who – as if on cue – had pulled out their phones. One such person was filming from behind, and I was sure my mosquito bite was so big it would be visible by Google satellite.

As I settled into my surroundings, I realised with a sudden urge that this was distinctly provocative. All the city's art collectors and who's who were in this very room, and I was the centre of attention. A couple leisurely embraced, and the woman caught my eye with a slow and knowing wink as her partner snaked his hand down her back to squeeze her buttocks.

The artist himself was a captivating sight to behold; his fingers moved deftly across the page. I forgot I was the subject and watched every stroke, entranced. When finished with a pose, Billich would flick his hand at me, a deft gesture that meant it was time to change my position. I found the movement devilishly commandeering. I surrendered willingly to each gesture, allowing myself to be beckoned with every whimsical motion.

I was relaxing now, and my imagination was running wild. At the end of the sitting I was enthralled to see the three sketches. They were all so beautiful. I grasped Billich's warm hand as I left. 'I am fundraising,' I said. 'Do you think we could work together?'

He agreed without hesitation, and thus a life-long friendship was born.

Over the course of the next five Valentine's Days, I went on a crusade. I had been able to reach Sir Richard Branson with my unique YouTube appeal; now I wanted to go one further. I knew the artform of burlesque was offering the same magic to my students as it was to me, and I hoped that by gaining support and endorsement from Sir Richard, we could take our message to the wider community and help more women. To date, the *My Heart Belongs to Branson* campaign has involved six cities, included over 250 people, and set seven world records. It was always a big collaboration and a shared achievement.

If Sir Richard Branson liked achieving the impossible, so did I. Meeting him became my mission impossible. I had a desire to prove to myself that I could scrape myself off the floor of a psychiatric ward and create a worldwide successful business venture. My primary purpose was to help people live with more fun and sparkle in their lives. I was here to share my joy.

All our videos for Sir Richard included volunteers and students from my burlesque network. I knew it was important to demonstrate the number of people feeling better about their bodies and enjoying their lives.

As the final weeks rolled around, we were still frantically fundraising. We also started a Kiss Petition. Instead of collecting signatures we collected kisses. We put up a poster saying, "Kissing Booth – $1 a kiss". People at our shows would line up to get their lips painted with lipstick, and then they would donate a kiss with their lip print on the poster, paying a dollar each time. I think we captured people's imaginations, because very generous patrons would even tip $50. 'You keep the change,' they'd say. 'Enjoy your trip to London.'

Sir Charles Billich also attended our events and donated sketches to the fundraiser. It was very kind, and I had to pinch myself. I had this talented man in my phone and willingly in cahoots.

Despite our best efforts, though, we only raised $1,700, which barely scratched the surface of the costs that lay ahead. Madame PR had her ear to the ground, and it transpired that Sir Richard was going to be arriving in Australia just weeks before we flew out for our Burlesque or Bust tour.

The biggest lesson in entrepreneurship came during the evolution of the *My Heart Belongs to Branson* campaign. I wanted to execute everything with utmost professionalism, and that meant investing money. I reasoned that a businessman like Sir Richard Branson would advise me not to spend on such a frivolous folly with no guaranteed return on investment, but the more I read books about Sir Richard Branson, the more determined I became. I found synergy between his drive and mine, and I wanted to connect, whatever the cost. I was particularly interested in his experience with Virgin Records, because in order to launch my own music I had decided to start my own label, Domina Records. I thought he would have valuable insight and contacts for the next phase of my evolution.

I decided I had to fly to Adelaide where he was speaking, to see if I could sing my song for him. Even better, perhaps we could play the *My Heart Belongs to Branson* video on the internal entertainment screen as he landed by plane. I called everyone – the organisers hosting the stage he was speaking on and contacts at the airline that had supported our tour. I wanted to see if they knew which plane he would be on and if I could get our video on the internal screens. It was all to no avail.

I was disappointed that the conference organisers wouldn't arrange for me to sing my song for him, but I thought I would be harder to decline in person. I had the logo on my poster to prove we were working with the airline, and I also had my poster with 300 kisses on it.

Weeks before our own massive trip from Melbourne to London and Bristol, I dipped into my dwindling savings account to purchase a trip to Adelaide, too. As I arrived at the event, I saw that it was a major conference and exhibition facility. I was wearing my full Australian flag costume and feather headdress to make sure that I stood out. Everyone was very entertained and wanted to understand what I was doing.

While I was happy to explain the story over and over, I knew these people weren't the right targets. With some nifty networking I located the head of security. He could see that I was a credible advocate when I showed him my poster and explained the airline's endorsement of my tour. And while it was impossible to meet my idol at that event, he took my number and texted me confirmation that a parcel had been put directly into the hands of Sir Richard's PA. I left knowing my mission had been accomplished; they had received my message.

In the end, though, my expedition – the Burlesque or Bust tour – was my greatest financial catastrophe.

I think, in hindsight, I should have been more careful about what I named the tour, because it really did send me bust!

As it turned out, I had to put the remainder of the flight money on my credit card. And when we arrived in London, we learnt that the first show had only sold 30 tickets. The second show was a total disaster – we stopped in Bristol only to be contacted by the major venue. They'd only sold six tickets and so they wanted to cancel the event.

I called back to Melbourne from Bristol with the news of this cancellation. I had to give notice on my flat and let my flatmate know to advertise my room. When I was returning to Melbourne, I would be moving back into my parent's home. I couldn't afford the rent any more.

For most people this kind of disaster would seem catastrophic. It could have even been a catalyst for another breakdown. But now that I had been sectioned and had fought my way back, I was built from thicker stuff. This financial collapse did not frighten me as much as a future spent without expressing my artistry. I had to express myself or I would go crazy. Whether or not I had money was of no consequence.

The flickering fire that had burnt within me as a small child had grown into a furnace. That little repressed lion dancer at Sunday School wanted her moment in the spotlight. Like Patrick Swayze's character said in *Dirty Dancing*, 'Nobody puts baby in a corner.' I wanted to be witnessed; I wanted to claim my lioness back. To this day, she is the root cause of my motivation and self-belief. I have risked many things other people would not. I have found an inner reserve and a resourceful and quick-witted approach to problem solving that I attribute to my overactive mind. I think creatively all the time. This is lucky, because I have to think creatively about how to get myself out of tight spots when things don't go to plan!

CHAPTER 12

YOU GOTTA GETTA GIMMICK

'I started my business on a G-string budget!'
Sapphira

Moving back home with my parents was a humbling experience, but it gave me the chance to come full circle. I began looking for new locations to teach my dance classes in their area. I found myself pulled back to The Ballet School, and to my surprise Miss Ballerina was still teaching there. She was still running the academy some 15 years later. We embraced each other with delight and she remembered my name. It was a lovely sight to see her surrounded with ballet costumes in the middle of the studio, trying to sort out the matching sets of tutus and their accompanying accessories!

'These are from a show we did last night,' she gushed enthusiastically. 'Oh, it is so nice to see you, I do love hearing of our students growing up and going on to do amazing things.'

I shared with her my escapades on the London burlesque scene and gave her a poster from my own dance academy. It was a way of commemorating the knowledge and joy of performing that she'd passed on to me. She was beaming. 'You know,' she said, 'we don't rent this space out for dance classes because we are owned by the council, but I have an idea. You should contact the Nova Music Theatre group. They have a studio that is often unused, and it's not far from here. In fact, the chap running it used to do our sound lighting way back when you were a ballet student here.'

I hurried off with the number, and I was intrigued when Mr Musical answered the call. 'You want to teach burlesque,' he said with a warm laugh. 'Now that's mighty coincidental, because we are just about to put on a musical about a burlesque artist. Do you know the musical *Gypsy*?'

Did I ever?! *Gypsy* was the story of the most famous stripper of her time in the burlesque world. She was known as Gypsy Rose Lee. I was blown away. I had started out in ballet at this small studio and now, 15 years later, I had travelled the world and returned to the same little block I grew up in. Here I was, linking up with a theatre group putting on a burlesque show. What were the chances?

I agreed to meet with Mr Musical to see the space they rehearsed in as a potential to hire for my burlesque classes. During our meeting another beautiful full-circle moment occurred.

'You know, we are actually in a bit of a jam with this show, *Gypsy*,' said Mr Musical. 'To be part of the show we need someone who can commit to all the rehearsals and someone just had to pull out. We happen to need someone to play a singing stripper,' he said.

I had to pinch myself.

I had a special skill on the burlesque scene. I would perform a "sing and fling" – a phrase I originally thought I had coined, but I realise that burlesque and singers have been around for decades, so I am pretty sure someone else came up with it before me! I was one of the few performers on the scene who incorporated singing into their act. In fact, some show producers would even ask me not to sing because they thought it didn't suit the burlesque style. This had always perplexed me, because the great Gypsy Rose Lee herself – years before our burlesque revival era – had made her mark using her voice. The spoken word was her signature performance style. Nonetheless, I was back in town and suddenly my luck seemed to be changing.

I told Mr Musical that I would love to be the singing stripper in *Gypsy: The Musical*. A few days later I found myself in front of the audition panel, and I got the part on the spot! It was the first time that had happened to me in my limited audition experience, but I knew it was a good sign. I could feel in my bones that I was going to nail this role and play it with all my heart. I was given the role of the unforgettable Electra, the stripper who used lights in her costume as her gimmick. I was also thrilled to see within the manuscript the title of the famous Stephen Sondheim song, 'You Gotta Getta Gimmick'.

It was awe-inspiring to read right to the bottom of the manuscript and see Gypsy Rose Lee herself listed as a co-writer. Knowing that my path was to cement my songwriting in the music industry, I felt touched that some 50 years earlier another burlesque artist and writer had been on the same path, especially one as renowned as Gypsy Rose Lee.

While I knew a little of Gypsy, becoming part of the musical about her life gave me intimate insight into the world she had lived in. She was originally in the shadow of her sister and had a pushy stage mother who was, in many ways, a frustrated artist in her own right. I realised that the routes that had brought her to the burlesque world were so different to my own. I empathised with the family's poverty and drive, travelling from theatre to theatre and living on a shoestring.

This script had fallen into my hands. It had found me rather than the other way around. It made me think of all the other times I had come full circle.

One in particular sprang to mind. As a young aspiring artist, I had worked in jobs to be close to my beloved artform. At 19 years old I was an usher in the Regent Theatre, a job I cherished. I would sell programmes and my favourite post would be at the top of the theatre, where I would turn on a torch and guide patrons safely. This spot was fantastic because I would get to see the whole show every night and have a little cosy place to sit, as the top step was behind all the audience rows. I drank it all in: the high ornate ceiling, the elaborate rows of plush red velvet chairs, and, of course, the performers. Deborah Byrne and Hugh Jackman were starring in *Sunset Boulevard*. Every night I would mouth the songs and lines along silently from that top step, wishing it were me on the stage. Many years later that dream would come true as I auditioned for the famous *Australia's Got Talent* with my dance troupe.

The auditions for *Australia's Got Talent* took place at the one and the same Regent's Theatre. Standing on stage in front of a panel which included Dannii Minogue was exhilarating and surreal. I thought of my original delusion of grandeur when I had imagined, in the psychiatric hospital, that I was being flown to meet Kylie. Now here I was in front of her sister, and every hair stood on end as I looked into her eyes to sing a beautiful song.

Although we were sadly buzzed off, I knew when we had finished that we had delivered a great performance. 'It was beautifully sung,' Dannii said. 'I wanted to make sure I said that.' What a thing to hear, after everything it had taken to get there. I was in ecstasy. Even more exhilarating was peering up right to the back of the theatre where I had once sat, wistfully wishing I was a singer in a fancy costume. It was a profound moment, one that I had to breathe in slowly. I was starting to realise my dream.

Now, as I was playing the role of Electra in this great musical, I was able to put a lot of the experience I had from stage productions like *Australia's Got Talent* into practice. Even the many small cabaret venues and private parties I had been performing at over the years had prepared me for being in a 14-show theatre run. As the opening right rolled around, the theatre company was abuzz. There were wardrobe fittings, extra rehearsals and, of course, the production of the show's programme. Remembering myself as the wistful usher dreaming about being up onstage, I was taken aback to see my own headshot in the programme along with a hugely talented cast.

We were accompanied in this musical by a 19-piece orchestra, and the big brass and percussion were electrifying. Oh, how I wished I could take them with me to every show! (I'm just not sure how I would fit them all on the back of my bicycle.) It added such a dynamic energy to have clash of cymbals, the toot of the trumpets and sweet sounds of the strings. The volume and timbre brought out the best performance in me.

The scene I performed in was backstage, and a timid Gypsy was thrust into the dressing room to meet her new co-workers. In fact, she found herself in the middle of a heated debate. A pair of veteran strippers, Tessie Tura and Mazeppa, were playfully arguing. But this struck a raw nerve. Although it was playful, it made me feel sad.

The fact is, it brought some less than joyful memories from my performance life back, and they haunted me. Although I was committing my all to burlesque in order to helps others find playful ways to combat mental ill-health, I had experienced some other mental health stresses on the path to becoming a more prominent artist. There were darker forces at work in the entertainment field. A small faction of the burlesque community had been bullying and trying to destabilise me.

As I had been working hard on noticing my own triggers, I was starting to see – with an empathetic eye – how others might also be triggered. I also recognised that they might not have the tools to unravel their emotional processes. I always did my best to be firm but loving. I wanted to keep my boundaries in place. But in truth, it was exhausting being the one at the top of the tree, always feeling like I had to keep my guard up to deflect jealous snipes and callous backstabbing.

I think that as a strong female leader – who was tapping into her prime sensual energy – I was evoking a lot of projections and negative reactions simply because of my skill with the media and my naked ambition. My goal was always to shine a light and help to share an artform that had saved me, but to those who did not know me I think I was misinterpreted and misunderstood. And while on the one hand burlesque was the crutch to bring my self-esteem into control after a mental health breakdown, on the other hand it has taken all my emotional training and skills to stay grounded and stable since becoming a full-time business woman in the arts industry, especially amid some challenging dynamics in a female dominated industry.

My philosophy is focusing on positivity and I chose to always see the best in others. But negative incidents happen to everyone. I want to shine a light and speak up in order to inform younger artists entering the industry. Bullying and sexual harassment can happen, so you need to be aware and speak up if you notice it happening to you. I have been sexually harassed by an inebriated lesbian bar owner at a show, who buried her face in my bosoms and blew a raspberry into my cleavage to show off to her friends. It left me feeling violated and unsafe and discriminated against by certain members of the gay community who questioned my sexuality and right to be within their environment.

I was also the victim of financial duress when female business partners – who paid a male counterpart promptly to preserve their reputation – took over nine months to pay my invoice when we ran the event without him the following year. I had invested savings into the business and he had not. After a sell-out show, I waited for four months to be paid by a club. When I was finally invited in to accept the payment, a wad of money to the sum of $2000 was held above my head and mockingly shaken just out of my arm's reach. They did this just to belittle me. It was a harsh lesson in the cruelty facing women in business, and particularly in the more unscrupulous and less regulated entertainment world.

When I met Miss No, she was a prominent performer who was renowned within a provincial scene. With my corporate sway, I had my portfolio beautifully presented in an A3 folder. As we met to discuss the biz, I opened each page to share the press I had secured in London. Although she smiled politely, I could see a serpentine flicker as her pupils narrowed to a slit. Her jealously was palatable. Not only was her body language toxic, it was the stench on her breath that made me uneasy. It was a dank haze of vile gas. I recoiled, but foolishly ignored my impulses. And then, almost as if I was being pulled back to my dark past, I later found myself at a show with Miss No. We were back in the dungeon-like cells of Club Danger.

Miss No hissed at me heinously, her fierce physique an immovable form. 'We don't want your positivity, Priscilla!' she spat at me with a stabbing staccato. I had a hard time learning to speak up for myself, and so I guess it was symbolic when I lost my voice for a year during this episode. Why the one very space – with its sinister, jail-like rooms – has been the location of two artistic crises, I will never understand.

Thankfully, these incidents have never outnumbered the sheer joy and blissful happiness that I feel when teaching a group of excited students or watching the post-show glow of my own dance troupe. Or when I watch my beginners when they come off stage to thunderous applause. 'There was more than just glitter at your showcases,' a student once told me warmly. 'Everyone's auras were glowing with pride.'

From Paris to Dublin, Plymouth to Pune, I have been welcomed and encouraged. And that appreciation has kept me going through thick and thin.

When, four years later, I finally succeeded in meeting Sir Richard Branson in London, it was at a conference for business leaders. The emphasis was on people creating change and disrupting industry. I felt encouraged to hear Sir Richard speak of his own failures in business, and many other leaders stood up to openly share how important it was not to let failure shake the spirit of young entrepreneurs, because it was such an essential ingredient to achieving success. I felt less ashamed about the fact our Burlesque or Bust tour had nosedived, not to mention the difficulties I had had as a single woman in business. In a way, the shame I felt about this failure was similar to the stigma I felt when speaking out about my bipolar episode. But the more I surrounded myself with like-minded people, the more I realised I wasn't alone. A lot of people had been through exactly the same thing. In this room of over 700 people, we all had similar stories to share. It was amazing meeting Sir Richard Branson at that event. I was grateful it was arranged by some very special people, because I worked so hard with a crowdfunding poem to get my ticket to hear him speak.

CHAPTER 13

WARRIOR'S DANCE

'There is a cry, a call deep within our hearts that wants to be heard. We long for the liberation of our voice and soul.'

Karina Schelde

When I resigned from my job to follow my dream and set up a business, I was embarking on an inner journey, too. *The More To Life* personal development courses were having an immense effect on my life. I could now be more masterful of my emotional reactions. I was able to pause when I was in the throes of fear or anger. I could then breathe and compartmentalise and put the incident aside until I had more time to process it with my processing book and tools.

The impact on my interactions day-to-day – at the bank, in the post office, or catching the bus – was improving immeasurably. My bigger personal-life relationships with family and loved ones were also presenting themselves in a new light, because I was so switched on to my triggers. I had solid remedies in order to untangle the quagmire in my mind.

I had also taken up other personal development work at the time of resigning. I was hungry for change. In a waiting room at a yoga studio, I found a brochure entitled *Soul Voice®: The voice is the most important instrument.*

I thought this might be like Gospel singing. I wasn't really sure. But I did know that whenever I sang I felt an energy shift in the room, and maybe this would help me explore how to use my voice to connect with people.

As I embarked on my first weekend, I couldn't hope to imagine what lay in store.

The course was taking place in an old church building that had been converted. Now it hosted alternative shows and educational events. We sat in a circle and had been encouraged to bring our own cushions, socks and blankets. I tucked myself into a little cocoon on my cushion and looked, in awe, at the striking woman at the tip of the circle. The image became emblazoned in my mind: her sitting on five tall cushions. She would become my guru, my mentor, my guide.

When the student is ready, the teacher arrives.

For eight years after this first encounter, I would be back in this position, sitting in a circle, learning from this amazing woman and following her all around the world. But as I sat tucked up at this first meeting, I did not know that this was what lay ahead.

Karina Schelde was the most extraordinary individual. She was here to help us release our voices. This was not singing. This was my warrior's dance.

We used our voices to express all our primal noises. We moved our bodies with raw emotion. Without using language, we were delving deeper into the layers of our subconscious. It was magical how powerful releasing anger and grief was when we did it together with her guidance and control.

I was intrigued to experience the Pain Release method. I had endured several broken bones as a child, and also when I was hit by a car crossing the road at age 13. These injuries healed, but

159

they had left me with frequent foot, ankle, and hip pain. My neck was also a constant source of irritation. If I was stressed I would develop neck pain. With the guidance of this teacher we were put into pairs and encouraged to locate the pain, look at what it really represented in our lives, and find a positive affirmation for that area or issue. Then our facilitator would make sounds and use touch to help extract the pain. When invited, we would also join in with our own voices.

As I watched Karina demonstrate the exercise, I didn't think it would work on me. I had pain in my hip and thigh where the car had struck me. Yet here I was, only moments later, in the deepest emotional release I had ever been permitted to exude. I screamed, cried, pummelled, and shrieked. I was surprised at the memories that flooded back when those areas were activated. I was very young at the time and close to the Brethren Church and their teachings. I realised I was storing a lot of panic in my body. I had supressed a lot of memories of that incident, of the moments the car had collided with me and my body had shut down, But when I began this process and started using my voice, some of the memories began to surface. I cried out.

As a child I thought that the accident was God coming to take me. As we worked on this memory 20 years later, the agony was still acute. My panic was activated as if I was reliving it right there and then.

This activity went on for nearly an hour, and afterwards I was utterly exhausted, diminished, spent. My facilitator stroked my forehead gently and sang soothing tones all over me. I drifted into a place of deep serenity and relaxation. When the session ended, I realised I was emptied of that horror, and something more wholesome was resting there in its place. Slowly my hip stopped hurting. I knew I had shifted something when my osteopath asked why I hadn't had an appointment for eight months. Prior to that experience, I had been going weekly! This was deep psychological work that was impacting on my physical wellbeing, and my voice was the way in. I was hooked.

CHAPTER 14

WILD FRONTIER

*'You don't learn to walk by following rules.
You learn by doing, and by falling over.'*

Sir Richard Branson – virgin.com

The Burlesque or Bust 2013 tour was the steepest learning curve of my life. Moving back to live with my parents was a lesson in unconditional love. I was a more resilient and caring daughter; my life experiences and living abroad had made me appreciate them all the more. I realised that they too had been shaped by their whole lives. They didn't have the emotional tools I had, so it was my duty to improve our relationship by working on myself.

I don't think I would be here without the love and support of my mother and father. They have helped me pick up the pieces, stored my belongings in their home and always been there whenever I needed them.

While I lost a lot of money on that UK tour, I gained something far more valuable. Bee-Loved was back in touch. He had broken up with his fiancée and we were speaking regularly. He was actually a key part of helping the Burlesque or Bust tour come to fruition, and he met me and the showgirls in Bristol.

I was now engaged.

It had been four years since we first met online, and there was no denying the flip-flops my heart did when I looked into his eyes. It was such a relief to have him back, and something else magical happened, too.

He had upgraded his studio and our tracks were being revived.

My voice had totally changed since I'd committed to the path with Karina Schelde's sound healing method. I now had a new command in my singing and spoken voice. Previously I would have conceded to please other people in group situations, but now I was speaking up for myself. This new authority came across when I sang. When we first turned on the microphones to record in our studio, the depth of my new voice and the combination of his new equipment was electric. We both beamed from ear to ear. We named the track we were recording 'Pussy La'. It's become my studio nickname and we use it with a wry smile every time.

The question was not a matter of "if" now, but a matter of "when" and "how". We were living in different countries. We knew we would be separated again, but getting engaged had strengthened our resolve. In London we completed the engagement by purchasing rings. Bee-Loved couldn't wait to call his parents to let them know I was soon to be part of the family.

When we said goodbye at the airport, we knew we were committing to this new wild frontier. And we were going to face it together.

Soon Bee-Loved became a face on my Skype again, as I was back in Melbourne. With the distance between us, the familiar pang tugged at my heart. I wobbled over the coming months and felt that maybe we couldn't survive a long-distance courting. To reassure me, Bee-Loved saved every penny – walking instead of catching the bus – to be by my side. He appeared in Australia with roses in his arms, sweeping me up and assuring me that he loved me and only me. When he visited Melbourne twice during the year of our engagement and reminded me of his love, I knew we would find a way no matter what the cost.

On his second trip to Melbourne we decided to seal the deal. I called to postpone his trip back to England and extend his flight. We had to give the registrar's office one day and one month's notice of our impending marriage, so we set the date: Friday, 4th July 2014.

My parents were travelling abroad and our decision was rushed, but those who could make it to a ceremony on the 21st of June would be invited to my final Sapphira's Showgirls Student Showcase where, at the end of the performance, Bee-Loved and I would share a commitment ceremony on stage as a precursor to the official wedding.

With three weeks to plan a wedding, I span into gear. It helped that we already had a venue and most of our friends were photographers. I assembled bridesmaid outfits from my costume collection and Bee-Loved hired a morning suit.

We performed together for the first time. He played piano and I sang a song I had written for him. As I looked across to smile at him during the song, my new voice soared up high into the sky, touching everyone in the room. It was not painful to sing high notes in my throat any more. And at the end of our vows, as our lips met, the room was fuelled with emotion. There wasn't a dry eye in the house.

The day of our official registry wedding rolled around soon, too. In my haste I had booked his return flight on the evening of our official wedding – it was a classic Priscilla blooper. Only moments after we said our "I dos", he would have to leave to be on a plane a few hours later. Saying goodbye to him at the airport after only just exchanging rings and a marital kiss was totally heart-wrenching.

This helped me make the decision to leave. I had nothing to keep me in Melbourne. My dance classes were drying up.

Burlesque had exploded across the city, and everywhere from yoga studios to pole dancing schools were now teaching the craft. The competition was catching up with me. My sister had given birth to twins and was now married in London, so there was little keeping me on home shores.

I found myself a temping job and saved for a few weeks. I began selling everything I owned to get some money together for our honeymoon. Little did I know that the temping job would become as pivotal a life-changing moment as any, as I was working at one of the world's biggest book publishers. In a round about way, this is partly the reason I am here writing for you now.

One month later I was flying overseas. This was my second cross-hemisphere romance, but this one felt right.

My suitcase was light and so was my bank account, but none of that mattered. I had found the one.

We met in Rome, the Eternal City.

We spent one night there, admiring the views.

But the next stop was the main destination.

We were flying to Ibiza.

We were going to see our idols, The Prodigy, who were headlining there. We were also going to stand on the shores of Café Del Mar, the place of the magical compilations with heart-stirring music. Together we planned to watch the famous Ibizan San Antonio sunset.

CHAPTER 15

IBIZA

'I write your name in the sand, jagged letters.
I write your name in the sand, do you remember?'

Summer Lust, Sapphira

"Ibiza is a beautiful, sun-soaked paradise based in the Balearic Islands of Spain. Since early history, Ibiza itself has attracted hedonists and freedom-seekers, from the Carthaginians in 654BC, to the hippies of the 1960s, to the clubbers of more recent times." (Bainbridge, 2010)

There is a mysticism to the energy and aura surrounding the island. There are volcanic properties in the rock which shape its foundation. There is no doubt that it is a magical place with a magnetic pull. It is hard to visit just the once.

As Bee-Loved and I landed at Ibiza airport, it was my second visit and his first. We had finished our album, and we couldn't wait to hear The Prodigy, the legendary band that had been so influential in the development of Bee-Loved's music production.

We made a list of artists and venues we wanted to see. I was in Ibiza with a business idea in mind. I knew the incomparable Dita Von Teese herself had been performing on the island, so it piqued my interest. For so long I had wanted to combine the exotic fashion and stage production of burlesque shows with the heavy beats of my foundation in dance music. Here in Ibiza, this combination was happening – and I was overwhelmed to see the exquisite high-end stage shows and exemplary production quality. The fashion and flair were abundant, and I had never seen anything like it.

As Bee-Loved and I made our way to Café Del Mar, the famous San Antonio sunset was about to light up the sky. We positioned ourselves on the rocks. I sat in front of Bee-Loved, who wrapped his arms and legs around me in a huge, comforting embrace. I knew I was safe here. I was home.

All the miles I had limped, galloped, and crawled in order to be at this place – in this very moment, with this beautiful man – had been worth it.

With Bee-Loved, my world was put to right.

Everything made sense.

This is what I was missing.

He looked at me with tenderness in his eyes. 'This is the mecca for dance music lovers,' he says. 'We've done it. Your album is written now.'

I gazed at him tenderly. Soft focus. Every time.

I thought back to the song that found me 20 years ago and smiled at him.

As you might have guessed, Bee-Loved is not his real name.

He is called Antony. But to me, like the song that saved me, he's just Tones.

CHAPTER 16

GET YOUR FIGHT ON

'If a large tree grows from this small seed we shall be grateful.'
Daniel Macmillan, 1843

I am here to take back what they took from me, and to help others who have had the same thing taken from them. The joy of sensuality and self-expression needs to be restored, in order to remedy so many mental health problems prevalent in society. My goal is to create a safe place in the entertainment industry, free from judgement, ego, and competitiveness, where radical self-expression can abound.

If we can attain unconditional self-love and encourage our inner artists – no matter what level of ability – to flourish, surely we are one step closer to attaining inner peace on our planet. I have taken up the mantle to do my bit, by nurturing one showgirl at a time.

To do this, I am taking up the mantle of forgiveness and connection, prising open the chasms in my heart where any latent resentment might still be contaminating my soul. This way I am free to stand on purpose as a teacher, leader and artist. It takes daily training to keep my mind clear, but my efforts have a visible effect in the way I communicate and the relationships I have with those around me, as well as impacting the opportunities that are now coming in.

I want to do more than shine a light. I want to be a laser beam of positive energy so bright, that onlookers reach for their sunglasses to combat the glare. If one person improves their own happiness and outlook on life, it triggers an immediate chain reaction of cause and effect. It is my mission to change the world by nurturing one showgirl at a time, until we have an army of positively powered people, uniting us all through a ripple effect of infectious love.

I sit here writing to you.

I have been called back. Back to The Spot.

Full circle.

It's been 14 years since DJ Real Deal's sister brought me here, but now I work here at one of the world's biggest book publishers. I have been saved. The foundation of this business is steeped in the preservation of history, lyricism, and poetry. I am being nurtured here. In the confusing and difficult periods of my life, words and melodies have always been a sanctuary and refuge. Within the walls of this publishing house, the heart that upholds a reverence for the written word beats strong. I have been embraced here and I feel at home. This is a safe place and I am being encouraged.

My writing has been mentored and my songwriting has been inspired. It is through contacts I have met here that I have been presented the opportunity to share with you, dear readers, my mental health story.

It is a tale called *Burlesque or Bust* because, without burlesque, my life is bust. I was broken, and I pieced myself back together.

The harrowing days of my youth are far behind me. Every morning I wake to the rise and fall of Bee-Loved's breath as I watch him sleep. I tuck my head into the crook of his shoulder.

I can't believe this vision lies beside me. I can't believe the comfort he has brought to my life. Every day begins and ends with 'I love you with all that's in me.'

He is my world.

Sometimes I go back to that scared, young girl, trembling and alone on the floor of the psychiatric hospital. When I am on stage about to sing; when I am standing in front of a group of new, excitable students in a dance class; when I am on the streets of Shoreditch covered in balloons to set a world record and raise money for mental health, I think of her. I stop and send love and vibrations from my dimension back to hers.

'Hang in there, little Priscilla,' I tell her. 'You are going to get through this. I know you feel alone in that room right now, but you are not. I, your future self, am here with you. I am here to tell you not to be afraid. You are going to achieve more than you ever thought possible. You are going to be a singer, you are going to record your album, you are going to meet the man of your dreams and the world's biggest business billionaire, Sir Richard Branson. I believe in you. You need to go through this. This moment here on the floor will put a fire inside you. You will use all the strength you get from surviving this experience to make yourself unstoppable when going for your dreams and starting a business. Above all, precious girl, you are going to do it. You are going to help thousands of people and be a bright positive light in a dull and dreary world. The world needs your light. Don't give up. Get your fight on.'

CHAPTER 17

SAPPHIRA'S SHOWGIRLS VALUES

1. Fun & Frivolity
2. Sister & Brotherhood
3. Team Work
4. Respect
5. Friendship
6. Outlandish Sparkle
7. Empowerment
8. Humility
9. Honesty
10. Forgiveness
11. Self-Awareness

I grew to learn more and more about Sir Richard over the five years I'd been pursuing him, and I realised that he had a lot of wisdom to share. He had set up mentorship programs within his businesses to help aspiring entrepreneurs. Since I'd successfully negotiated a business discount through my Valentine campaign, I continued to reach out to him to learn more. I felt I could do even more by entering competitions like Pitch to Rich, which I did in 2016. It was a UK-wide search to find the nation's brightest entrepreneurs. Of course, I had inadvertently been "pitching to Rich" with my *My Heart Belongs To Branson* campaign, but it was incredible to me that there was an actual Pitch To Rich campaign in which I could win up to one million pounds in prizes – including a trip to Necker Island!

I finally met Sir Richard Branson at the #VirginDisruptors event in 2016. It was a conference for "People Creating Change". When I heard that Sir Richard would be in town, I thought to myself, I am not going to think *I can't afford it*, I am going to think, how can I afford it? And thus the idea of the crowdfunding poem came into fruition. Armed with my trusty Bee-Loved at my side, we fired up the home studio and recorded the poem. My own campaign, *My Heart Belongs To Branson*, had dried up all my funds, and it was with the caring support of others that I was able to attend as everyone chipped in a little bit to help me get there. When I reached out to friends and family across the globe, I felt a real warmth and love as each little donation came sailing through. I know that most of these people will probably read this book, and finally understand why I've been so driven about my burlesque business and sharing this artform with the world.

When the staff at the event asked me to stand to one side for a picture, I thought they meant to have a photo by myself. It was only when I looked up and saw Sir Richard in front of me that I realised they meant for us to be in a picture together! I would at last shake his warm hand and look at his friendly face. I shared the press and stories I had achieved in the time I had been trying to reach him.

'Well done you,' he said with a caring grin.

At that moment I actually froze and was lost for words. I also cursed the fact that my Australian flag corset had a faint musty smell from being kept in a drawer for too long. What would Dita do, sweeties? I have been a colourful addition at many business events while wearing my Australian flag attire; I am usually the only showgirl in a room full of suits. It's a good thing I'm not shy, darlings!

To this day I feel sheepish that – in order to keep the affiliation with Sir Richard Branson's airline since the day our first video launched – I paid for the tickets on my credit card and transferred the balance to Sir Richard Branson's credit card company soon after.

As it happens (don't tell anyone), I am still paying it off!

So in a way, he did help me finance it.

Now I just need to pay him back.

Sapphira meets Sir Richard Branson at #VirginDisruptors in London, October 2016.

HOUSE OF MACMILLAN

House of Macmillan, you saved me
Lost but with glee now am found
Pen's humble servant and guardian
Bid to say, sing or write each word down

I've travelled where're it's commanded
Without choice am at its behest
With bittersweet journey near broken
Found a place for sweet moment of rest

Your walls echo forbearer's greatness
Disciples same covenant bound
The expanse of this mantle is carried
Like a baton between each passed down

Though tears taint the ink of each letter
Our bloodline a quest to complete
Restless we with ageless labour
Each word births its shape on the sheet

House of Macmillan, host glorious
I'm at your table to dine
Shoulder to shoulder the authors
Brothers and sisters of mine

Nourish our souls with your bounty
Guard us your fortress so bold
Deep in your archive a treasury
Parchments more precious than gold

A troubadour's path I was wandering
At times in my heart so alone
Yet, House of Macmillan you saved me
For your house to many is home

For James Waller
By Priscilla "Sapphira" Silcock

ACKNOWLEDGEMENTS

There are so many people to thank, so please indulge me these pages.

Firstly, thank you to my husband, Antony Silcock, who is life's greatest gift. I would also like to acknowledge the many hundreds of people and volunteers who have supported me over the years, but in particular my parents, Alan and Maria, my sister Jessica and her family, my mother-in-law, Hazel, and brother-in-law, Danny. My Aunty Eva deserves a special mention here, as she has been by my side as a constant source of support, buying most of the raffle tickets at my events, and providing financial and emotional help whenever I needed her.

In loving memory of my Opa, Oma, Pop and Nan. All members of the Legg family, the Sitlanis, and the Loidls, my extended relatives.

My dear friends Penny Kee, Pia, Heathy Myers, Adeon, Nathan Thomas Jones, Hana Vraniqi, Dave Bamforth, Bigsy, and Sam Illingworth.

I would not have had the rich experience in business and the crazy antics we have created without the Sapphira's Showgirls community, and I give a huge sparkly thank you to Maryanne Taggart and Rochelle Felstead.

The secret garden who let me borrow their summer house to write this novel, thank you!

RMIT University, Blacky High School and especially Paul Edwards and Meg Stuart.

Personal thanks to my editor, Stephanie Cox, for being so patient, and never-ending thanks to James Waller, who has been a true friend and comrade.

To Milan Wilenga, for his mentorship, and to my business mentors Darren Loidol, Paul Burns, Clive Herbert, Glen Williamson and Pam Morris. Sir Charles and Christa Billch, whose generosity knows no bounds, plus the kind Joy Casey at Billich Gallery for all her help.

To Dame Stephanie Shirley, whose vision of empowering women in business is inspirational. Jan Turner and everyone at the Nova Music Theatre group. My beloved More to Life community, founded by K. Bradford Brown and Roy Whitten.

Particular thanks to Issy Crocker, Steb Fisher, Bill Thatcher, Clare Vivian-Neal and Suzanne Loubris.

To the various teams at the Virgin Group, in particular, Anna Catchpole, Vito Anzelmi, and Emma Masters.

My friends in publishing who gave me invaluable advice Jaime Marshall, Tara Anderson, Emily Lawrence, Helen Caunce, Ursula Gavin, Suzannah Burywood, Emily Birolini, Margret Szymczyk, Amanda Woolf and Clare Ruel.

I have made many friends in the colourful world of burlesque, and so here I want to thank Sharon Kay at Burlesque Baby, Helen at Siren Doll, Zelia Rose, Louise Rio Wild of Miss Pinup UK, Saph Rox of the UK Burlesque Awards, Jo King of the London Burlesque Academy, Marianne Cheesecake, Dominique DiVine and Ephipany DeMeanour at Dublin Burlesque Festival, Velvet O'Claire at Burlesque Stripped Down, Eva Valentina at Burlesque Moulin, Lady May, Kylie Lavery at Dancemakers, Claire Phipps at Flaming Feathers, Ministry of Burlesque, Jamila Wardknott, Sassy La Showdoll, Matteo Cruciani and the warm-hearted Sammy Dodger.

I would not have grown without the support of kind venues, including Red Bennies, The Greyhound, Barry and the team at La Dia Da, and Juliet and Lia at Juju's Bar and Stage. My dear friends at Dizzy's Jazz Club and the Roger Clark Quartet. José, Brigette and Claudia at HEART Ibiza, Diego Calvo and Concept Hotel Group, Dawn Hindle and Lisa Faichy at Ibiza Rocks, Arnaud Lauris and Sabine Pena at La Bella Ibiza, and Silvia Reissner at Le Crazy Horse, Paris.

I would also like to give thanks to:

Karina Schelde, for her amazing Soul Voice Method®, and my international sound tribe. To the Palacios-Banay and Kelton families, who have taken me under their wings at various times.

To all the photographers who have helped me illustrate my vision, but especially Lisa Law, Lara Blake Gourley, Lucas Ranzuglia, Zeljko Krncevic, Alex Martin, Matt Kent, Marco Joe Fazio, Rebecca Horley, Jesse Spezza at Beckon Media, and Len Panecki. To the amazing filmmakers Mark Bakaitis, Remo Camerota, Jeff Osman and James Alexander.

To the dance studios Ross House and The Space Dance and Arts Centre.

To the women who have inspired me as a performer, including Dita Von Teese, Immodesty Blaize, Gypsy Rose Lee and Azura, as well as those who paved the way in the music industry: Kylie, Alison Goldfrapp and Madonna.

To my big sister in show business, Di Rolle. My kind friends Helen Anderson and Lara Brockhurst at Anderson Brockhurst, Cali Crawford, Albert Murcia, Daniel Whitsett and Michael Bjerregaard at Secrets in Lace, Marie Delon at Marquis de Sade, Alexandra Gill-Chambers at Clockwork Butterfly, Ros Helmut at Australia Wide, Todd and Stephanie Prather at Pastease®, Fiona at Bettylicious, Sarah Thomas at Circus Ibiza, Nick Stacey at Vinacecous, Nina Clavant and Tom Winch, Mike and Charlene at Rock N Romance, Vivien of Holloway and all the sponsors of my calendar but a special mention to Lidia at Sweet Pins and Kornelia's Kloset. Thank you to

Warren Gooch for his generous donation of feather fans and costumes.

To the make-up businesses and hairstylists who helped me create my alter-ego, including Julian Kynaston, Joanne Poskitt Suzanne Rizk, Giselle, Cindy at the MUA team at Illamasqua plus Trudi Netherwood, Donna Billing at Hair Extrodonnaire Susan Swartzberg, Ksavi, Edvin Mac, Shiene Mann and Mischel Vounatsos Bratsos.

To all those I cherish in the music industry, Spencer Baldwin, Anthony and Luca, Isadora Van Camp, Mark John, Danny D, James Bragg, Kristian Townsend, Doc Moody, Gary Eccles, Emilio Merone, Michael Hull, Lee Martin, Robert Upward, Tony Mantz, Alex Virr, Mark Pember, Mark Brown, Gigi Canu, Alex Neri, Marco Baroni, Marc Durif, Alexander Nettlebeck, Rory Clark, Aaron Mellor, Recardo Patrick, Maxim, Ted and Kerry Woollan, and in loving memory of Sergio Della Monica.

A heartfelt thanks to my singing teachers, Dominique Oysten and Lisa Perks.

To Liza Dezfouli and Edd Moore at the Plymouth Herald for their great coverage.

To Mario Piutti, Oumesh Sauba, Darren Sanicki, and Moira McKenzie.

To my Islington Angel, Kathy. To Thom and Oli – a song of thanks.

To my crowdfunding supporters including Pam Loidl, Duncan Mundell, Michael Stenhoj, Sarah Hall, Will Abdo, Coco Demure, Rebecca Levene, Lucy Jay, Susie, Kurt Spencer Rowe, Richard, Louise Owen, Thanh Dang, Anderson, Anthony Pappa, Dominique Werny, Jonathan Rowbury, Judy Patootie, Kerry Wollard, Cristian, Pad.A, Becky Miners, Jennifer Lynn, Lauren Karl, Moana, Manuela Cocchi, Benjamin Coppel, David Leigh Dodd, Victor Albert, Boogie Rose, Peter Lurie, Geraldine Park, Aaron Smiles, Alicia Wallace, Alison Gomez, Julia Shaw, Ally Finnan, Amanda, Abby Skye, Sarah Stanton, Kristen Dorian, Sandie Cook and Karen Butler.

RESOURCES

Sapphira - Mistress

You've read the story, now listen to the music.

www.sapphiramusic.com

Connect with Sapphira online at all the pages below:

www.facebook.com/sapphiramusic

www.instagram.com/sapphiramusic

www.twitter.com/sapphiramusic

SAPPHIRA'S SHOWGIRLS

TESTIMONIALS FOR
SAPPHIRA'S SHOWGIRLS

www.sapphirasshowgirls.com

Sapphira's Showgirls classes are supportive in helping people explore their inner showgirl. A light-hearted, bubbly personality shows testament of overcoming the stigma of mental health, which becomes overlooked in theatrical arts.

Karamela Deusa

Like most girls, I've had body confidence issues forever, never skinny enough, boobs too small ... bum too big ... you name it. It's so fantastic to see all shapes and sizes celebrated and proud of their femininity.

Fleur Tayshus

I'm so passionate about burlesque; it's addictive! I was a shy, mousy girl before, and now I have the confidence and courage to be the woman that I truly am.

Sadie Soho

Learning burlesque has been one of the best things I have done. Burlesque is empowering, sexy and an art form. It does not discriminate and is extremely expressive.

Lolita Stray

Well written and full of emotion ... Priscilla's eagerness and enthusiasm shines through.

Jo King, London Academy of Burlesque

REFERENCES

OPENING QUOTES FOR WAKE UP CALL AND SKYLINED:

Dr K. Bradford. *Guidelines for an Inner Journey,*© Lifetimes Press, lifetimespress.com

IBIZA PARAPHRASING:

Bainbridge, L. (2010) *The Guardian.* Available at: www.theguardian.com/music/2010/jun/27/ibiza-party-spirit (Accessed: 04/04/2018).

OPENING QUOTE FOR "GET YOUR FIGHT ON"

Morgan, C. (1943) *The House of Macmillan.* Daniel Macmillan to Archdeacon Hare, 7th March 1843 from 57 Aldersgate St. London: Macmillan & Co.

10 PRINCIPLES OF BURNING MAN

Harvey, L. (2018) *The 10 Principles of Burning Man.* Available at: https://burningman.org/culture/philosophical-center/10-principles/ (Accessed: 02/07/2018).

MORE TO LIFE:

©K. Bradford Brown PhD. 1983. All rights reserved. More To Life was created by K. Bradford Brown, Ph.D. and W. Roy Whitten, Ph.D., as a way to offer others the skills and practices they developed through their work in psychotherapy and pastoral counselling. All processes mentioned are protected by copyright and cannot be reproduced or taught without written permission.

**If you found this book interesting ...
why not read this next?**

Sex, Suicide and Serotonin

**Taking Myself Apart, Putting Myself
Back Together**

When Debbie Hampton took the mix of wine and drugs that
nearly killed her, she didn't ever want to wake up – but she did,
and her problems were only just beginning. In this book,
Debbie tells the inspirational story of how she forged
a new life for herself.

Love and Remission

My Life, My Man, My Cancer

Annie Belasco had everything except a man. When she found
a lump in her breast, her life seemed to topple over.
But though she was facing mortality at such a young age,
she didn't let it stop her from finding love ... and remission.

A Series of Unfortunate Stereotypes

Naming and Shaming Mental Health Stigmas

Drawing on her personal experience with anxiety,
Lucy Nichol tackles a number of different stereotypes placed on
people living with mental illness with wicked humour
and a dose of 80s sparkle.

the *Shaw* **mind**
FOUNDATION

Creating hope for children,
adults and families

Sign up to our charity, The Shaw Mind Foundation
www.shawmindfoundation.org
and keep in touch with us; we would love to hear
from you.

We aim to end the suffering and despair caused by mental health issues. Our goal is to make help and support available for every single person in society, from all walks of life. We will never stop offering hope. These are our promises.

TRIGGER™
The voice of mental health

www.triggerpublishing.com

Trigger is a publishing house devoted to opening conversations about mental health. We tell the stories of people who have suffered from mental illnesses and recovered, so that others may learn from them.

Adam Shaw is a worldwide mental health advocate and philanthropist. Now in recovery from mental health issues, he is committed to helping others suffering from debilitating mental health issues through the global charity he co-founded, The Shaw Mind Foundation. www.shawmindfoundation.org

Lauren Callaghan (CPsychol, PGDipClinPsych, PgCert, MA (hons), LLB (hons), BA), born and educated in New Zealand, is an innovative industry-leading psychologist based in London, United Kingdom. Lauren has worked with children and young people, and their families, in a number of clinical settings providing evidence based treatments for a range of illnesses, including anxiety and obsessional problems. She was a psychologist at the specialist national treatment centres for severe obsessional problems in the UK and is renowned as an expert in the field of mental health, recognised for diagnosing and successfully treating OCD and anxiety related illnesses in particular. In addition to appearing as a treating clinician in the critically acclaimed and BAFTA award-winning documentary *Bedlam*, Lauren is a frequent guest speaker on mental health conditions in the media and at academic conferences. Lauren also acts as a guest lecturer and honorary researcher at the Institute of Psychiatry Kings College, UCL.

Please visit the link below:

www.triggerpublishing.com

Join us and follow us...

@triggerpub

Search for us on Facebook